Praise for

"Jeffrey Lloyd in this insightful examination of the ethos of our society has done a national service by reminding a generation of who we are, how far we have come, and the level of discipline and commitment that it took to bring us where we are".

His Excellency, the Honourable Wendal Jones, Bahamas Ambassador to the United States

"A true testament of the power of resilience, Jeffrey Lloyd offers us an inspiring tale that it's not where you come from, but what you come to."

Most Honourable, Dr. Hubert A. Minnis, former Prime Minister, Commonwealth of the Bahamas

"Jeffrey Lloyd is an inspiration to me."

Hercules Granger, Executive Director, The Hope Center; Rayne, Louisiana, USA

"A Leader who lives from the heart."

Christopher B. Maxey, Founder, Cape Eleuthera Island School; Eleuthera, The Bahamas.

"A mesmerizing chronicle of life's remarkable adaptability and the metamorphosis of an enduring soul, artfully fusing intellectual richness with elegant simplicity and a dash of wit."

Dr. Showalter Johnson, Mentor to the Super Rich, Founder of the Billionaire's Roundtable

"The personal mission and soulful experiences of Jeffrey Lloyd's life inspire and uplift the reader to never be wary in their journey, no matter how bleak and challenging it may become. The hand of God, coupled with the personal work required for self-realization is well worth the effort, because in this journey of determination is where joy and beauty are found."

Dr. Jeffrey McNairy, Medical Director, Rythmia Life Advancement Center; Guanacaste, Costa Rica

A JOURNEY OF HOPE

A JOURNEY OF HOPE

TRANSCENDING BOUNDARIES

A TRANSFORMATIONAL TALE OF RESILIENCE & PERSISTENT FAITH

JEFFREY L. LLOYD

UNIVERSAL IMPACT PRESS

Copyright © 2023 by Jeffrey L. Lloyd

All rights reserved.

No portion of this book may be reproduced in any form without written permission from the publisher or author, except as permitted by U.S. copyright law.

Scriptures taken from the Holy Bible, New International Version®, NIV®. Copyright © 1973, 1978, 1984, 2011 by Biblica, Inc.™ Used by permission of Zondervan. All rights reserved worldwide. www.zondervan.com The "NIV" and "New International Version" are trademarks registered in the United States Patent and Trademark Office by Biblica, Inc.®

Scripture quotations taken from the (NASB®) New American Standard Bible®, Copyright © 1960, 1971, 1977, 1995, 2020 by The Lockman Foundation. Used by permission. All rights reserved. lockman.org

This memoir is based on the author's personal experiences, recollections, and perceptions. While every effort has been made to portray events and characters as accurately as possible, some names, dates, or details may have been altered, anonymized, or composited for privacy and narrative fluidity. The views and opinions expressed within are those of the author and do not necessarily reflect the official policy or position of any other agency, organization, or individual. This book is not intended to serve as a source of legal, professional, spiritual, or therapeutic advice. The author and publisher disclaim responsibility for any inaccuracies, errors, or omissions, and neither is liable for any damages, whether incidental or consequential, stemming from the use of, or reliance on, the information within this memoir.

Book Cover by Arete Media International.

Published by Arete Media International, under the Imprint "Universal Impact Press" www.AreteMediaInternational.com

Paperback ISBN: 978-1-956711-27-1

Hardcover ISBN: 978-1-956711-39-4

This book is dedicated to my Grandmother Leta Lloyd.

Preface

The unfolding journey of a soul, its growth, and metamorphosis, resonate more profoundly when recognized and endorsed by those who walk beside it – parents, siblings, friends, and a diverse network of societal connections.

This tangible affirmation is a reflection of the celestial approval each of us is destined to receive, encapsulated in the divine affirmation: "This is my Son, whom I love, and with him, I am well pleased. (NIV)"[1] Without this endorsement, psychologists caution, a soul potentially treads a path veiled by self-doubt, misguided loyalties, a delicate self-image, and a diminished sense of self-worth.

We voyage through the undulating sea of life, guided by the signposts of our unique environments. These landscapes are carved by the rich mosaic of our personal experiences within the small world into which we are born and nurtured. Fortuitously, this personal cosmos expands beyond our immediate kin, gracefully embracing a constellation of 'foreign bodies'—an intimate web of neighbors, friends, and, on occasion, the most unlikely of acquaintances.

My narrative, too, is crafted by such dynamics — a tale shaped by the realities of poverty, deprivation, and constricted possibilities, yet consistently uplifted by the divine grace of God. Throughout my voyage, an undercurrent of hope sustained my unyielding resilience.

My life story emerges as a testament to optimism in the face of adversity, a beacon of invincible hope for a brighter dawn, which, though often shrouded amid uncertainty, was steered by the omniscient and ever-present hand of God.

The symphony of my existence was enriched by a choir of souls, to whom I owe an immeasurable debt of gratitude: my parents, siblings, relatives, friends, neighbors, educators, colleagues, chance encounters, and even those seen as 'adversaries'. The stories that unfold in this book offer a glimpse into the vast spectrum of experiences that collectively weave the intricate tapestry of my life — a life that inspires humility and profound gratitude within me.

As we embark on this journey together through the pages of "A Journey of Hope: Transcending Boundaries - Tale of Transformational Resilience and Faith", I invite you to dive into the depths of my experiences, trials, triumphs, and the indomitable spirit of adaptability that defines my existence. May you find resonances, lessons, and most importantly, a reason for hope within these pages.

1. Matthew 3:17 (NIV)

Contents

Prologue	XVII
Introduction	1
SECTION 1: Roots	3
1. Originators	5
2. Grand Dame	11
3. Early Years	17
SECTION 2: Social Awareness	23
4. Cognitive Awareness	25
5. Formative I	29
6. A Prejudiced Society	35
SECTION 3: Education	39
7. Formative II	41
8. Eastern Junior	47
9. Big Red Machine (SAC)	51
10. College Years	69

SECTION 4: Self-Discovery		83
11.	Work Life	85
12.	Marriage 1.0	99
13.	Divine Awakening	107
14.	Homeward Bound	117
15.	Marriage 2.0	123
16.	Fatherhood	135
17.	Marriage - Vehicle of Self Discovery	139
SECTION 5: Public Persona & Commitments		145
18.	Media	147
19.	Diaconate	153
20.	SERVOL	159
21.	The YEAST Rises	169
SECTION 6: Public Advocacy & Spiritual Evolution		189
22.	Law	191
23.	Jaya One	197
24.	Partisan Politics	209
Epilogue		221
About the Author		231
Acknowledgements		233
Fullpage Image		235

Prologue

"A Journey of Hope: Transcending Boundaries – A Tale of Transformational Resilience and Faith" presents an exhilarating expedition through the trials, tribulations, and triumphs of the human spirit. Authored by esteemed Bahamian Jeffrey L. Lloyd, this narrative dives into his multifaceted life, offering readers a unique exploration of personal growth and plasticity.

From modest beginnings in the sun-drenched islands of The Bahamas to the pinnacle of socio-political achievement, each chapter reveals a significant life lesson. This book serves not only as a memoir but as a watchtower, casting light on life's potential even amid adversity.

Through his intimate reflections, Jeffrey challenges the conventional concept of 'normalcy,' demonstrating inherent optimism and an unwavering spirit of possibility. Painted on the canvas of his life, he skillfully portrays essential lessons on forgiveness, durability, gratitude, and the transformative power of change. His account of persistence, pliability, and community strength forms a relatable and realistic narrative that captivates, inspires, and enlightens.

"Journey of Hope - Transcending Boundaries" is a remarkable testament to the human spirit's capacity to rise above circumstances and achieve greatness. It serves as an inspiration for those seeking self-discovery and purpose.

Embark on this inspiring journey and discover your path to transcending boundaries. This book is not merely a recollection of life experiences, but an invitation to activate your innate capacities, grasp the essence of forgiveness, and unleash the cathartic power of change.

Let the journey begin.

Introduction

L IFE IS A GRAND orchestration of faith, an evanescent ripple in the infinite, timeless fabric of the cosmos. Its terrestrial significance and quintessence are meticulously carved by the sociocultural and anthropological context that envelops it. Value, in the grand scheme of life, arises not from isolation but from the complex web of relations with individuals and circumstances.

In this memoir, my existence unfolds against the sun-kissed backdrop of The Bahamas. The shifting landscapes of life, the cultural nuances, and personal trials and triumphs intertwine to shape the lens through which I viewed my earthly sojourn. Particularly vivid in my memory are the existential patterns I intricately wove in the heart of Kemp Road and Fox Hill, New Providence; the quietude of Roses, Long Island; the cow-grazed lands of Shawnee, Oklahoma; the vibrancy of New Orleans, Louisiana, and countless personal journeys.

In these pages, I invite you on a journey through my life, one that began with few material possessions but was rich in social ties. A strong sense of camaraderie and community, combined with an ingrained culture of care, respect, and genuine concern for others, served as a reliable compass that guided my life's journey. Akin to these transcendent qualities was the permeating sense of resignation often found among some Bahamians: one that, in many cases, translated into surrendering of personal future to unseen external forces, which meant drifting along life's currents, filled with trials, hardships, joys, and victories, and carried towards an inevitable destiny.

These forces often found shelter in societal institutions - churches, lodges, burial societies, bars, and pool halls - influencing life's trajectory. Born into this social fabric, I, a child of single parents, Eltoy Louise and Stanford Leonard, ventured to carve my unique path. Despite the limitations presented by my parents' prematurely halted education and constrained employment opportunities, I was determined to chart a different course.

Through it, I acquired a collection of hard-earned lessons and native wisdom, providing a framework for navigating life's complexities. I appreciated the importance of industry and self-respect, the perspectives hidden in every mistake, the liberation found in forgiveness, and the boundless power of gratitude. Through it all, I discovered the essence of appreciating the journey rather than the destination, the potential in every life, and the necessity of personal change.

ROOTS

CHAPTER ONE

Originators

My mother, a radiant, beautiful, brown-skinned woman, was the cherished youngest child of Alexander and Lurie Taylor. The limited educational opportunities of the time brought her formal schooling to a close at the tender age of fourteen. Shortly after, she became a 'Monitor,' essentially an untrained teaching assistant. She was the final one of her siblings to journey from the tranquil serenity of Long Island to the bustling vibrancy of Nassau, enticed by the promise of a 'better life.' This generational pilgrimage was eased by elder siblings who had blazed the trail earlier, nurturing their younger kin and acting as 'parents' during the transition phase. Their guidance was not merely a kind act but an obligation mandated by their island-born parents, who upheld the societal norm of older children caring for the younger ones. This was the reality of my mother's early days, sheltered under the roof of her eldest sister, Violet.

My father, on the other hand, was the eldest offspring of Leta and Wesmond Lloyd. He, too, like my mother, followed the well-trodden path of familial migration, with him embarking on the journey several years before my mother. Women from the islands typically sought employment as domestics, while their male counterparts journeyed to the town to 'learn a trade,' venturing particularly into the construction industry. My father began his journey with land surveying, a skill he honed and utilized throughout his career. Meanwhile, my mother earned her livelihood as a domestic worker.

The mid-twentieth century witnessed The Bahamas, along with many other Caribbean Islands ("CARICOM") and Commonwealth countries, as colonies of Great Britain. A march towards self-determination was initiated during the '40s, '50's '60s, and '70s, with several CARICOM nations like Jamaica, Trinidad, and Barbados attaining independence during the 1960s, while others, like the Bahamas and Grenada, achieved this status in the 1970s and beyond. As British "subjects", we found ourselves navigating a cultural landscape that largely conflicted with the native, African heritage indigenous to the slaves that crossed the Atlantic and adapted to its new environment. While the indelible imprints of European imperialism and colonialism were powerfully etched into our social fabric, the residue of the African culture such as agricultural work and savings schemes like the ASUE remained ensconced within the hearts and minds of the liberated Africans.

The imposed foreign influence eventually sparked a wave of rebellion during the 40s, 50s, and 60s, led by a growing contingent of conscious Bahamian activists who protested the discriminatory and socially devaluing conditions forced upon the common Bahamian. The expanding awareness of human rights, self-determination, and social equality burnt bright in many hearts during these tumultuous years. Within these passionate 'liberators' was a call for greater participation by black Bahamians in their country's economic, political, social, and cultural spheres. These aspirations were amplified by revolutionary speeches of influential leaders like the late Sir Lynden Pindling, Clarence Bain, Dr. Doris Johnson, Mary Ingraham, Randol Fawkes, Sir Etienne Dupuch, Henry Milton Taylor, and many others. My mother, though quieter, was an equally fervent participant in this crusade for greater Bahamian involvement.

She held views starkly different from those of my father. They both harboured profound concerns about the world in which their children – myself, brothers, Charles and Rodney, and later, sister Christina - would inherit. Yet, it was my mother who risked economic ostracization and possible unemployment through her covert support for the nascent Progressive Liberal Party (PLP), founded in 1953 by her political mentor and dear friend, Henry Milton Taylor. Her alignment with the PLP's cause mirrored the sentiments of her politically awakened contemporaries, a protest against the deeply ingrained prejudices that shackled the progress of individuals like her – young, black, and female. Driven by the encouraging words of Mr. Taylor, her involvement symbolized a collective yearning for transformative change in the lives of her countrymen.

She looked inward, examined her life, and decided that she didn't want her children to endure the same trials she had faced. By the time the PLP was established, she was already twice a mother, with both me and Rodney nestled in our familial cocoon.

My father Stanford, on the other hand, though politically astute, held a more muted and contrasting stance. He was a staunch but silent supporter of the predominantly white United Bahamian Party (UBP), not risking being labeled as a radical dissenter despite his private remarks among friends that the 'black man can't run this country'. As a child, I observed these diametrically opposite political loyalties with curiosity. Raised primarily by my father and his mother, my paternal grandmother, I was doomed to imbibe some of his political perspectives and worldview, if not his inherent predispositions.

To be fair, my father wasn't alone in his belief about the governing capabilities of the 'black man,' nor his support for the UBP. Many black Bahamians echoed these sentiments. I'd heard it straight from their mouths. They had their justifications, of course, because many were employed by white-owned firms, including my father who worked at Obrien Engineering. Preserving the status quo meant them exhibiting perceived cultural traits of the average Bahamian: 'docile, friendly, and agreeable'. My father, too, was averse to causing any sort of upheaval.

At the same time, he was undeniably a 'mama's boy'. My grandmother, Leta Lloyd, a woman of robust build and indomitable spirit, possessed an unparalleled candor that made her an imposing presence. Perhaps it was this characteristic that led my mother to entrust my upbringing to her when I was just two months old – a story for another time. My father's worldview was unquestionably shaped by his mother's attitudes. His parents' separation, coupled with a strained relationship with his father, a black man like himself, likely pushed him into an overly protective stance toward his mother.

This was not unusual amongst young men of that era, who venerated, if not deified, their mothers. They were the family's backbone and ever-present figures in a child's life. Many, like my own, were single. While fathers may have been involved, it was usually from a distance. It was mothers who bore the brunt of child-rearing and home-making. This explains why anyone who dared to criticize or insult a person's mother risked a severe, if not violent, backlash, a treatment not usually extended to insults against someone's father. Single parenthood did not begin in the 60s or 70s, contrary to what some Bahamians believed. Both of my mother's sisters, for example, were single parents. In my case, this family configuration placed me primarily under the care of my dominant grandmother, who influenced my life just as much as she did my father's.

Chapter Two

Grand Dame

While my biological parents represented one thread of my lineage - noteworthy, unique, and irreplaceable - the true parental influence in my life was Grandmother Leta, a woman of singular worth, whom I affectionately called "Grandma". My upbringing was not particularly unusual. Many children, like me, benefitted in their formative years from the gentle yet firm hands of grandparents who viewed this as an opportunity to invest in their future. For some, it offered a second opportunity to 'do it right', while others regarded it as a cultural necessity to aid their city-dwelling descendants. Others, though, possibly calculated it as a move to prepare suitable companions for their twilight years.

Regardless of her motivations, Grandma probably considered raising me as a way of discharging a debt she owed my father - her eldest and beloved son, who sacrificed his entire life to ensure her well-being and comfort. In a tangible sense, Dad never quite severed the umbilical cord. He lived under the same roof as his mother for his entire adult life.

Grandma was a woman of tremendous dignity, albeit with modest resources, who personified the proverbial axiom: "cleanliness is next to godliness", as eloquently professed by the renowned John Wesley in the eighteenth century. Despite not parading her Christian virtues ostentatiously, she was deeply ingrained with age-old values of respect, trust, kindness, benevolence, self-control, and veneration for all life. She was an incredibly disciplined woman, who insisted that I ingest the same ethic.

It is remarkable that despite exiting the formal education system at fourteen, as mandated by the laws of the time, she wrote weekly letters to her children, living in the 'out islands'. She penned these letters with such a flourish of beautiful cursive and near-flawless English, exhibiting syntactic and literary coordination that would provoke envy in the average modern high school student.

She was profoundly rooted in the oral traditions of her ancestors, often aligning her life's perspectives and disposition with the wisdom encapsulated in an 'old saying' or aphorisms. Unbeknownst to me at the time, many of these adages subconsciously formed the foundational blueprints of my mental architecture, shaping my worldview and approach to life. I can still hear her voice in my memory, repeating:

"A stitch in time saves nine" or "As you sow, so shall you reap" or "If you spit in the wind, it blows back in your face" (her favourite), or "The early bird catches the worm" (her usual justification for waking me at the crack of dawn every day, including weekends) or "Mouth could say anything, takes money to buy land."

Her most frequent refrain was, "Don't mind the noise in the market, only watch the price of the fish", which seemed to be a shield she adorned against the occasional verbal attacks and criticism that were sometimes leveled by her own family. She was a pragmatic, disciplined woman with rigidly established habits.

As I grew, I sensed her struggle with what I perceived to be a deep-rooted, intrinsic shame. At random moments, and without any apparent trigger, she descended into prolonged periods of melancholy, marked by bouts of inconsolable weeping. No one seemed to understand the origin of this grief. Perhaps it was the 'dishonor' of being born out of wedlock, a fact she often lamented. As the daughter of an unwed mother, Margaret 'Muggie' Watson, she frequently recounted how, tainted with the 'bastard' stigma, she and her mother were subjected to relentless ridicule from relatives and neighbours.

It also could have been the scorn she endured for marrying Wesmond Lloyd, a black man, in an era when such unions were an unspoken taboo. The insidious shadow of racism did pervade amongst some native Long Islanders, including members from both sides of my family. Like Leta, my maternal grandmother, Lurie, was also shunned by her family because she married a black man, my grandfather, Alexander Taylor. Several of her brothers died without ever speaking to her again after the marriage. Despite this ostracism, my grandmothers defied societal norms and birthed numerous children with their husbands, demonstrating a willingness to bear whatever societal price their choices attracted.

Grandma's melancholy may have also stemmed from the fractured family life she endured, coupled with the lingering guilt and regret from a divorce, and the ensuing loneliness that often accompanies such circumstances. I later learned that the separation from her husband was particularly bitter, causing a schism among her children. I discovered that it was her domineering nature and occasional caustic language towards her husband that played a part in their estrangement. However, my grandfather was not without fault either. He was notoriously derisive and quick to berate and insult anyone who crossed him. Uncle Allan once told me that upon leaving Long Island, he declared he would not return to "these Long Island dogs". Presumably, it was this, among other possible reasons that, of all her children, her eldest son, Stanford, remained steadfastly devoted to her.

Growing up in The Bahamas in Grandma's era was indeed a formidable challenge. The struggle for survival was a daily task, forcing inhabitants to carefully strategize for each upcoming day. Despite these hardships, I occupied a privileged position. I was Grandma's sole responsibility, and she showered me with unwavering devotion. Up to her death in 1977, I was her world's axis, the focal point of her every waking moment. In return, she was the bedrock of my life, an ever-present figure with whom I shared almost every single day during the first decades of my life.

Her annual visits to her children in the 'out islands' are etched indelibly in my memory. One such trip in the mid-1950s was particularly heart-wrenching. During this journey, she spent two weeks visiting her daughter, Ethlyn, in Andros. Two weeks for a young child felt like an eternity. It was one of the few times that I stayed with my biological mother, who told me later that each day of those two weeks, I stood by the roadside, scanning the horizon north and south, tears streaming down my face as I cried for my Grandma's return. My inconsolable grief either so irritated my mother or evoked such compassion that she sent an urgent telegram (the prevalent mode of communication for pressing matters at that time) to Grandma, imploring her to come and "get this child", which Grandma did.

In those days, family members returning from trips abroad, particularly the United States, were celebrated by kin and neighbors as near celebrities. Crowds flocked to these 'homecomings' to inspect the returning travelers' belongings, discern any changes in their appearance, and listen first-hand to their travel anecdotes. Such was the grandeur of my grandmother's return.

It was a Sunday and she sat on her bed, consoling me as she shared her experiences. The healing of my fractured heart had finally begun, but the pain was still nearly unbearable. Tears of relief mixed with the lingering sorrow streamed down my innocent face. My source of comfort, my beacon of stability had, during her 'interminable' absence, been cruelly yanked away from my grasp. But now, she had returned, reinstating a sense of normalcy in my world.

"I will never leave this child again," she vowed, her voice tremulous with sobs. The pain mirrored in her eyes was as tangible as my own. And just as shockingly, for she seemed taken aback by the depth of my desolation.

True to her word, she never did. Throughout my upbringing, she remained my rock, providing me with the wisdom, love, and care that shaped the person I am today. Even though she grappled with her internal anxieties, never let them interfere with her mission - to raise me with love, discipline, and an unyielding spirit, just like hers. She was, and remains, my beacon of resilience, and the embodiment of selfless love.

Chapter Three

Early Years

Although I was born on the balmy shores of New Providence, the delicate mosaic of my formative years was woven on the rugged terrain of Long Island. One fateful tale my mother shared with me was of my grandmother's joy on hearing of my birth. With a heart brimming with love and her arms open wide, she swept me up, barely two months old, from my mother and returned to Long Island, where I was nurtured and raised.

This revelation - a jigsaw piece in the sprawling puzzle of my life - began to weigh heavily later on my adolescent mind, prompting the pressing question one afternoon, "Why?" The oddity of it caused tremors of confusion to ripple through my being. "Why," I wondered, "would a young mother, cradling her infant for the first time, willingly relinquish her precious bundle to someone who, despite being her lover's mother, was essentially a stranger?"

"You don't know Leta Lloyd, eh?" my mother would counter, her voice laced with a quiet, steady tension, especially when her fears or anxieties were prodded. My insistent probing on this particular day only heightened her discomfort.

"That was normal during those times," she continued, vainly attempting to mollify my burgeoning curiosity. "It was customary for the elders from the out-islands to come to Nassau, collect their grandchildren, and return 'home' to raise them. This was your grandmother's tradition too."

To my parents and grandmother, much like other out-islanders, Long Island was 'home' - a term that held an emotional resonance unmatched by Nassau. The land of their birth was a radar, commanding their hearts to visit regularly, reuniting with kin still rooted in their homeland. My persistence, however, only grew. "Why was I the one chosen?" My frustration swelled, casting an accusatory shadow on the possibility of my brothers being the so-called 'sacrifices' instead. It was clear that my mother, my beloved 'Toy', was taken aback by this unexpected confrontation. She had considered this custom to be so ubiquitous, that it had never warranted further contemplation. Moreover, my sudden emergence as a discerning, questioning young adult caught her off guard. Her lack of preparation was symptomatic of her inability to comprehend my irritation, frustration, and veiled anger. To her, she thought she had done what was 'right' at the time.

The stark retrospect of this situation unveiled the illogic of her decision to me. Yet, as she later revealed, I was an unwitting 'victim' (and beneficiary) of the social construct of that era. Despite the difficulty it posed for me, this ***was*** the norm and it was accepted - though, admittedly – with some struggle on my part. My grandparents, like their peers, were stewards of vast tracts of land. They eked out a humble existence through farming and cattle rearing. This generational handover of children to grandparents was usually born out of necessity: young city-dwelling parents were often cornered by financial constraints or a lack of reliable childcare options or both. The islands offered a supportive network of relatives and neighbors, a far safer, more nurturing environment than the bustling city life ever could. Despite modest means judged by urban standards, islanders enjoyed freedom from the burden of urban living expenses such as rent, utilities, and motor transportation.

This early separation meant that I only truly came to 'know' my biological mother *as my mother* later in life when I was about seven or eight years old. Memories of intermittent stints with her in my early years emerged like fragments of a dream. Residence with my grandmother remained virtually uninterrupted until my high school graduation and embarkation on the collegiate journey in 1969, a chapter of my life that I will delve into in the following pages of this memoir.

Knowledge of my early separation from my mother occasionally ignited sparks of discontent between us, straining our relationship and infusing it with an uncomfortable tension. This shadow from the past cast a pall over our interactions, its complex emotions difficult to navigate. The crux of my struggle with this early life 'picture' was two-fold: On one hand,

I grappled with the idea of a young, first-time mother surrendering her newfound joy to a 'stranger', relinquishing not just her newborn, but also the precious, intimate, day-to-day interaction that forms the cornerstone of a mother-child bond. This concept left me stunned, particularly as I began to comprehend the crucial importance of such early bonding between mother and infant. On the other hand, my young, innocent mind was unable to decipher the cultural intricacies of the time, or fully comprehend the formidable personality that was my grandmother. This 'irritation' persisted for several years. Even my siblings couldn't fathom this simmering, barely concealed anger towards our mother. They thought it was triggered by a 'forced' relocation from my grandmother's home to live with her as I prepared for college. But their assumption couldn't have been further from the truth; my resentment ran much deeper.

The path to understanding and acceptance was long and arduous. Yet, through thoughtful introspection and emotional healing, I gradually realized that my mother's decision was a manifestation of her love for me, and her desire to safeguard my best interests. She and my grandmother distrusted the seemingly 'treacherous' environment of New Providence, favoring the idyllic tranquility of their Long Island home. They believed that this would provide the safest and healthiest environment for me to grow and thrive. The presence of a doting grandmother was merely a bonus. As time would prove, their decision for me was the right one. My upbringing on Long Island was steeped in care and discipline, a privilege I cannot emphasize enough. While far from being spoiled, my life was shaped by my grandmother's undivided attention towards my welfare, safety, and proper upbringing.

As I matured and grew spiritually, I began to perceive this series of events as a pact I made with the Universe before my earthly incarnation. I was destined to absorb the austere simplicity and introspective essence of island life. I understood that I had come to this world to realize my divine self: a being perfectly congruent with God, the Supreme Being, the Ultimate Reality, the Source. I understood that my parents, my grandmother, and the Long Island community, with their simple traditions and values, were meant to shape the foundational ethic of my life. Core characteristics such as honesty, hard work, peacefulness, devotion, discipline, and a shared sense of community were ingrained in me, thanks to Leta Lloyd and Eltoy Taylor. By divine agreement, they served as conduits to my cosmic realization, a mission they executed flawlessly.

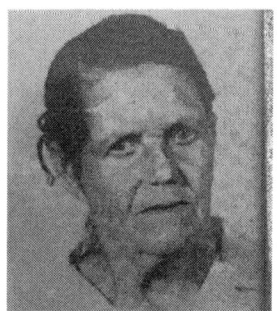

Grandmother: Leta Lloyd

Mother: Eltoy Taylor 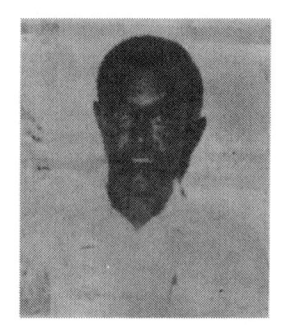   Father: Stanford Lloyd

Ancestral Home
Kemp Road, Nassau

SOCIAL AWARENESS

Chapter Four

Cognitive Awareness

On the surface, I was no different than other young lads my age, immersed in the rambunctious revelry and innocent mischief of childhood. However, beneath that youthful exuberance, my soul craved something deeper: meaning and purpose in life that extended far beyond the superficial.

My initial spiritual instinct awakened in me a desire to accept Jesus Christ as my personal Lord and Savior. At different times, I considered becoming a Minister of the Gospel or even a Priest. But the yearning was more profound than that. A sense of cognizance deep within me whispered that there was more to our terrestrial existence than the mundane realities of daily life. I chased this undefined passion for transcendence with a steadfast determination, guided by the lighthouses of religion and an uncompromising stand against conflict, deceit, and violence.

My quiet longing did not go unnoticed by those around me, particularly my grandmother, although it was occasionally overshadowed by the overpowering cultural norms of our times. I was required to attend Sunday morning services at the Protestant Church of God on Fowler Street, and Sunday evensongs at St. Margaret's Anglican Church on Kemp Road. Under the sacred arches of these sanctuaries, my desire to be *'cleansed by the redeeming blood of Jesus Christ'* assumed greater intensity.

The fervor to become a 'Christian' was so potent that I remember praying with a passion every night for a 'dramatic conversion'. This desire was fueled further by witnessing similar transformations in some of my contemporaries, like my childhood friend and neighbor, Mary Ellen Nairn. Her devout Christian expressions were stimuli that inspired my spiritual journey. There were others too - the late sister Gertrude Fox and the late Felix Miller, to name a few, whose lives epitomized sanctity, reverence, and an unshakeable faith in God. Their captivating spirit and benevolent nature were powerful incentives for me to tread the same path.

My moment of salvation did come, however, in a way I could not have foreseen, and much later than I had hoped. As my inclination towards this divine calling became more evident, even my mother occasionally hinted at picturing me in the robes of an Anglican priest.

One particularly memorable occasion stands out. The raucous cries of a male itinerant preacher, backed by a fervent ensemble of 'prayer warriors', interrupted my slumber one weekday night. The school night routine was that I would retire by 9 p.m. to prepare myself for the ensuing day's chores before heading off to classes. However, on this evening, Grandma roused me from my half-asleep state to observe the animated preacher and his followers from across the street.

Traveling preachers were frequent sights in my youth. They often gathered under streetlights for the benefit of curious onlookers. The preacher would claim to be "sent" by God to deliver a "word to His people," in this case, the people of Kemp Road and its vicinity.

On this evening, during his sermon, he singled me out from the crowd, summoning me to join him. This filled me with dread as everyone, including myself, expected that a "word from the Lord" usually meant a reprimand, a public denouncement of the sinful life one had led up until that point. As I crossed the deserted street, my legs trembled and my heart pounded against my ribs as I approached the fervently passionate preacher. His presence, fueled by a spiritual zeal, had worked his assistants into a state of religious trance. As I obediently but fearfully drew near, he placed his shaking hands gently on my head.

"Son," he began, his voice barely rising above a murmur, while the audience watched with bated breath, "You will be a great man one day," he faltered. "But you have to change your ways of living," he finished, leaving a pregnant pause in the air.

At that moment, I sensed countless eyes on me, mirroring my understandable trepidation. Once completed with me, he shifted his attention to call upon another bystander, I let out a breath I didn't know I was holding and retreated to my spot. The preacher continued, declaring his 'word from the Lord' upon one onlooker after another.

That episode left an indelible imprint on my memory. His words became a reason for hope, a prophecy that reverberated in my mind from that day forward. Throughout my life, similar words were repeated by various 'prophets' in different circumstances.

The identity of the preacher remains a mystery to this day. I left the meeting on unsteady legs, certain that I was a changed young man and knew that I would awaken the next morning 'saved', or deeply regretful of not being so. Little did I know, the process of salvation had only just commenced.

The persistent desire for ordination that underpinned my early life led to many heartfelt conversations and moments of discernment with anyone whom I felt could offer guidance or help me unravel this divine 'call'. Sometimes, it was my youth pastor at the Fowler St. Church of God, the late Rev. Felix Miller. At other times, it was Monsignor Preston Moss, whom I first met one afternoon at the cross of the new St. Augustine's campus 'down below'. I sought his counsel on deciding whether to become a Catholic Benedictine monk or a diocesan priest. I can't recall the advice he gave, but whatever it was, it did little to alleviate the alternating periods of tension and calm that characterized my spiritual journey for many years after.

CHAPTER FIVE

Formative I

"YOU WANT SOME SOUP?" Grandma asked. "Yes, Ma'am", I replied, barely able to contain my anxiety as she, Dad, and I prepared for our annual trip 'home' to Roses, Long Island. The mailboat, Air Pheasant, was our usual mode of transportation, which made weekly trips between Nassau, Long Island, Inagua, and Rum Cay carrying passengers, freight, and mail.

The Bahamian mailboat system, both past and present, functions as an economic lifeline for island communities. Each weekly voyage unfolds into an exciting spectacle, an event marked in every islander's social calendar, stimulating whispers and conversations that last long after the departing waves have settled. The passengers, usually relatives or familiar faces, provide fuel for the community's chatter, their arrivals and departures serving as an intricate potpourri of stories for days and weeks on end.

My family's financial circumstances, coupled with Dad's peculiar reluctance, steered us away from air travel. Despite his modest earnings,

I suspected that a seed of negative self-worth circulated within him, potentially convincing him that he was undeserving of the seemingly luxurious airline travel. He had a habit of downplaying his achievements, dismissing his hard-earned status as a qualified surveyor, a profession that demanded an exquisite blend of intellect and expertise. His keen observation and critical analysis of the Bahamian political, social, and economic landscapes got lost in the shadows of his unassuming demeanor. The origin of his feelings of inadequacy remains unknown to me, yet this self-perception was not entirely uncommon among his peers. To my later realization, some fragments of these self-diminishing paradigms had seeped into my subconscious, subtly molding my worldview and discernment of self, and possibly sabotaging a greater degree of my achievement and success.

A few tentative spoonfuls of the lukewarm, bland soup were all I managed before resting the bowl in my lap, sparking a fire in my grandmother's eyes. "I knew you didn't want no soup," she retorted, her irritation palpable as she snatched the enamel bowl from my grasp. The mostly untouched, cold lump of Campbell's vegetable soup lay in the bowl much as she had served it mere moments ago. My appetite was certainly present, but, the thrills of our upcoming Christmas journey to Long Island eclipsed any desire to wait for the soup to be heated on our humble, two-burner kerosene stove.

After an eternity of waiting, we finally embarked on our journey to the dock, where the Air Pheasant was moored. The 19-hour trip to Long Island was a long one, the boat heaving under the weight of provisions and expectant passengers. The anticipation of our yearly Christmas visit was mirrored by our island family, who anticipated the arrival of our bountiful supplies of food, clothing, and tools. My father, ever the provider, ensured that we brought more than sufficient supplies to last our stay.

Pivoting Schools

The frequent oscillation between Nassau and Long Island meant that my school attendance varied between Roses All-Age School, St. Margaret's Church School on Kemp Road, and later Eastern Prep School on Shirley Street. I was enamored with the idea of 'returning home,' to be among my paternal kin. Long Island was a cocktail of excitement and adventure - a setting Grandma, too, favored.

She remained unconvinced by the allure of a permanent residence in Nassau. The brisk pace, an inkling of danger, and the less-than-welcoming aura of the capital city came with a steep emotional discomfort. While Nassau may have served as an attractive destination for shopping and brief sojourns, she was drawn to the familiarity and tranquility of her native island. The predictable rhythm of life, the genuine warmth of close-knit community ties, and the peace of her origins, where she birthed all her children, provided a comforting anchor. She had honed the craft of survival in these parts, juggling farming, fishing, plaiting, and homemaking, despite a life largely separate from her husband. This state of flux defined my early childhood, alternating between the two islands, until a final shift occurred in the wee hours of January 9th, 1961, when I disembarked the Air Pheasant in Nassau for the final time. A fresh chapter of my life had unfolded.

Eastern Prep, the institution where my academic journey took flight, is seared into my memory. Interestingly, the criticisms directed towards today's educational system — the lack of male teachers, the dominance of female teachers, and the scarcity of resources and materials — mirrored the conditions of my time. My parents recognized the metamorphic power of education, viewing it as the primary vehicle for their children's upward mobility. Despite achieving literacy by fourteen, formal schooling ceased for them at that age. 'Learning,' as they put it, extended beyond the realm of law and obedience. It was about 'making something of yourself' — a mantra I heard often.

My early teachers were all females, including the Principal, Mrs. Armbrister, supported by a devoted team of educators like the then Miss Judith Pratt (later Mrs. Sherwin Thompson), Ms. Edgecombe, Mrs. Smith (who taught us numbers), and Ms. Wilson, who captured my young imagination with her radiant beauty and her patient lessons on writing the alphabet.

The school was a thriving hive of learning. Classes were often conducted under the shade of a sprawling tree in the yard, sans the familiar trappings of blackboards, textbooks, libraries, or labs that are commonplace today.

Despite what may appear to have been a deficiency, we never felt deprived. The fundamentals — reading, writing, articulation, arithmetic, teamwork, and respect for our elders and each other — were all nurtured there.

The early years also inaugurated, in addition to behavioral and attitudinal characteristics that frame the mental paradigms of one's life, relationships that formed the bedrock of one's lifetime social pillars. Eastern Prep was the meeting ground for one such encounter. From our initial engagement, the twin brothers Arthur, Otto, and I became instant friends – a connection that not only deepened since but has become the central non-biological bond of my life. Their parents – Bert and Leila – were like my parents; their sisters and extended family, virtually my own as well. No matter the pathway we took, our mutual involvement was understood, expected, and assured. From those early pre-primary days to now, we have been inseparable.

I loved school, not least because of my inherent curiosity. As an only child of the household, I created my own universe of recreation, fun, and knowledge. Solitude and silence were my treasured companions. Countless hours were spent frolicking in the yard, observing insects, playing games, and shooting marbles solo, spinning tops, or assembling 'box-carts' from discarded pram wheels. The simple pastime of riding up and down the traffic-free Kemp Road filled my days with endless joy and amusement.

Chapter Six

A Prejudiced Society

Within the contours of my early childhood, the Bahamian society was woven with threads of social, economic, and political complexities. The harsh realities of this stratified society compelled students like me to extract nuggets of inspiration from the unfailing commitment of our teachers and venerable elders. The backdrop of a discriminatory and socially challenging environment remained a silent spectre, hovering beyond our youthful consciousness.

My father, a man deeply engrossed in the captivating politics of his era, engaged in spirited political discussions with anyone willing to lend an ear. This birthed within me an abiding interest in the unfolding narrative of Bahamian society. As I grew, I was introduced to the prevalent racial attitudes of the time. Black people, simply because of their skin colour, were barred from employment in the bustling stores of downtown Bay Street or the elegant Savoy movie theatre nestled there. Miraculously, however, the barbed arrows of prejudice never grazed me. I shared classrooms and friendship circles with white students, companions who navigating our academic journey together. George Albury, Jay Simms, his sister Maxine, and Godfrey Roberts, are names that easily tumble from my memory. We spent countless hours in playful banter, sharing lunches, and walking home, arm in arm. I remained untouched by the faintest inkling of bias from them. Godfrey, particularly, was a cherished confidant, and his family extended their warmth and affection towards me.

Intriguingly, despite the enormity of societal injustices, I recall no major outcry or uprising among the Bahamian populace. Apart from the 1958 general strike, my memory holds no defining imprint of any citizen-led resistance against these entrenched societal deprivations. I perceived no noticeable discontent with the prevailing 'status quo' amongst the average Bahamian. It seemed as though most were resigned to accept their circumstances.

However, as time marched on, I came to understand that there did exist a parallel narrative. Other Black Bahamians, refusing to kowtow to the status quo, were tirelessly labouring to alter the societal landscape. Dynamic legal minds like Randol Fawkes, Lynden Pindling, Arthur Hanna, and Paul Adderley, alongside a cadre of freedom fighters, diligently orchestrated activities designed to awaken the collective consciousness. These endeavours culminated in Bahamian women securing the right to vote in 1961, an achievement born of the suffragist movement. This movement, while not explicitly feminist, served the objective of electing men to the Parliament.

The pursuit of civil rights, racial equality, and economic parity, which began to gather momentum in the early '40s, reached a crescendo on a day termed "Black Tuesday," April 27, 1965. Before this watershed moment, modern Bahamian political history was marked by the Burma Road Riots of June, 1942. This incident erupted from the demands of Bahamian labourers for equal pay, irrespective of colour or nationality, and was followed by the 1958 general strike initiated by taxi-cab drivers and the 1961 victory of women's suffrage.

According to historical records, on Black Tuesday, the ruling United Bahamian Party proposed an Order to establish boundaries for the various constituencies of New Providence and the Family Islands, as per the 1964 Constitution. In the ensuing parliamentary session, the PLP proposed two amendments to the Order, designed to garner a fairer representation of the electorate and their distribution. Both amendments were summarily dismissed. It was then that Lynden Pindling, then Opposition Leader, approached the Speakers' table, and seizing the 165-year-old mace—an emblem of parliamentary authority—declared, "This is the symbol of authority, and authority on this island belongs to the people and the people are outside."[1] With a flourish of rebellion, he cast the mace through an open window to the awaiting throng below. The act was lauded by the PLP as a "deviation in the pursuit of liberty and fairness."[2]

Curiously, my father was absent from the House of Assembly on that momentous April day. He was gainfully employed by a white Bahamian civil engineer, Gordon Obrien. Having sharpened his professional skills in England, Obrien returned home to found an Engineering Firm. In the hierarchy of the company, my father rose to the position of a foreman and, through a combination of grit, determination, and self-study, became a proficient land surveyor. His job required him to spend lengthy periods away from home, working in the Out Islands, laying out roads, docks, bridges, airports, subdivisions, and more.

Due to his professional obligations, my upbringing fell largely to my grandmother. Her discipline, often administered under the looming threat of a 'beating' from my father upon his return, was underscored by her favourite, albeit foreboding refrain, "I ga tell ya Pa, just wait." Although she did occasionally 'cut my behind', my fear of her disciplinary tactics gradually waned over time. As the years passed and the islands developed, my father's absences became less frequent and of shorter duration.

As a child, I was oblivious to the political and social tumult unfolding around me. My parents and teachers shielded me, and my peers, from the injustices suffered by black Bahamians. Life, as we knew it, felt ordinary. Whether they were protecting us or themselves—fearing economic repercussions from the white oligarchy—I cannot say with certainty. Yet, these early experiences planted the seeds of my journey towards understanding the complexities of my homeland's history and social fabric.

---

1. 2015: PLP - 50th Anniversary, Black Tuesday, Lest we Forget

2. Ibid

EDUCATION

Chapter Seven

Formative II

"**F**ALL IN LINE," MRS. Armbrister's voice boomed, snapping our scattered, juvenile focus into a sharp immediacy. It was a gathering of eager seven-year-olds, bidding farewell to Eastern Prep and stepping onto the threshold of Eastern Junior School. The physical path between these two establishments spanned an entire mile along the quiet, barren Mackey Street. In a testament to the times, there were no parents or caregivers, as there would possibly be today; but instead, shepherded by our teachers. The spring air of 1961 carried no lingering sentiments of tearful goodbyes or jubilant graduation ceremonies. There was a stoic absence of rituals marking this transition.

To my knowledge, none of my classmates had ever set foot in Eastern Junior before; there was no hum of excitement marking the change. In our conservative society, we were pliant to the rules, submissive to the dictates of our elders, which was extended to all authority figures - teachers, police officers, clergy and beyond. Marching in synchronized harmony along the scarcely crowded Mackey Street, hardly seemed a formidable cognitive exercise to us. It was a mere extension of this compliance.

At Eastern Junior, the esteemed Edwin Dawson Conliffe held the reins as Headmaster. My tenure at Eastern Prep had ably equipped me with the essential academic skills of reading, writing, and computation. The journey that followed, at Eastern Junior and St. Augustine's College, only further developed the robust scholastic foundations and discipline previously instilled by Eastern Prep.

Throughout my early school years, I was often a leader in class activities, running errands, and leading in various ways. The 'chosen' child, as I was fondly referred to. Our primitive education system lacked a structured method of selecting class leaders, leaving the responsibility to the subjective judgments of teachers and administrators. Thanks to my 'natural' leadership qualities and impeccable diction, I was viewed as extremely intelligent, and a reliable executor of tasks given me. And I would rise to the occasion, delivering with meticulous precision.

My articulate speech often earned me the curious label of being 'American', a term loaded with tacit admiration. My unusual eloquence was regarded as impressive and uncanny for a native-speaking child, leading some to erroneously perceive me as pretentious. I was clueless about what the 'American' label entailed, a fact that puzzled both laymen and authority figures alike.

An instance of this misunderstanding unfolded during a carefree afternoon spent frolicking in a sand pile on a vacant lot opposite my Kemp

Road home. The owner, on his sudden arrival, chased us away, leaving me without my shoes which he took to the nearby Police Station. Hoping to retrieve my shoes, I made my case fervently to the officer stationed there. My eloquence, instead of aiding me, was met with skepticism and a rebuke: "You 'tink you is American eh? Boy, come out dis station." Again, confronted by this 'American' phenomenon, I only knew I had to recover my shoes, or face Dad's wrath. Over time, the 'American' label lost its weight, and my eloquence was acknowledged as a gift, paving the way for my future success.

Despite my ignorance of the 'American' label, Bahamians, in general, held the United States of America in the highest regard. This fascination stemmed largely from the late nineteenth century, with many Bahamians traveling there, particularly to South Florida. In the early 1940s, Bahamian young men were actively recruited to work on "The Contract" or "The Project".

According to the Bahamas Department of Archives, the "Contract" was an agricultural labour program, launched on March 16, 1943, as a joint initiative between the Bahamian and U.S. governments.[1] Under this scheme, thousands of Bahamians toiled on American farmlands, cultivating and harvesting a plethora of crops. From the sun-ripened peaches of Georgia, the golden cornfields of Minnesota, Florida's citrus groves, to the peanut farms of North Carolina, Bahamians left a footprint across the American agricultural landscape.

Though many Bahamians eventually returned home, a considerable number laid down roots in the US, primarily in Florida and New York. This exodus had a profound impact on Bahamian society. Marking its 50th anniversary in 1993, "The Contract" was celebrated for its transformative role in the lives of countless Bahamians.

In a rich discourse with my friend Cordell Thompson, a former official at the Ministry of Tourism and an authority on the program, it was evident that "The Contract" had many positive social and financial implications for Bahamians. It presented an opportunity to gain invaluable agricultural skills and experience. Likewise, the eminent Bahamian historian, the late Dr. Gail Saunders, underlined the enormous economic and societal influence that the program had on Bahamian families.

The influx of remittances from contract workers led to the establishment of numerous local businesses, infusing new energy into the Bahamian economy. From small-scale shops and gas stations to laundry services and construction trades, a business revolution took shape. Although the program underwent several modifications, it remained intact until 1966.[2]

Dad was a also participant in "The Contract", spending several years in Kissimmee County (Orlando), South Florida, picking oranges. His reminiscences of the experience were sparse. In fact, many families in Kemp Road had relatives who had journeyed on "The Contract", some of whom never returned home, including my maternal Uncle Melvin.

American culture, thus, was a potent influence in The Bahamas for several decades, predating my birth and continuing into the present. The allure of the American way of life, with its seemingly superior standard of living, captivated many young Bahamians like myself. The towering skyscrapers of cities like Miami and others, the whirlwind of fast cars, and the intriguing lifestyle, were visions that filled our youthful dreams, shaping our aspirations and worldview.

---

1. 2010, The Bahamas Folklore Collection, Director, Cordell Thompson

2. Ibid

CHAPTER EIGHT

Eastern Junior

My journey through Eastern Junior was marked by moments of profound awakening, much like the biblical reference of 'coming to oneself' in Luke 15. As the year 1963 approached its twilight in December, the teachers decided to stage a Yuletide performance, the timeless classic, "A Christmas Carol." My flair for oration, a characteristic at times misunderstood and ridiculed, was precisely what the teachers sought when selecting me for the starring role as Ebenezer Scrooge.

On the day of the performance, an excited crowd of eager elementary school students, teachers, and staff, filled the central campus building. As the spotlight of the show, I graced each scene with my presence. I can still recall the vast sea of faces that beamed with anticipation as I made my initial entrance onto the stage. The cocktail of nervousness and exhilaration threatened to overwhelm me, but with a commanding self-assurance, I calmly narrated my meticulously memorized lines. My expressive, assertive tone and impeccable diction sent ripples of excitement through the young audience, causing Mr. Conliffe to intercede many times, urging the students to settle down so other actors could be heard.

That performance catapulted my profile throughout the school. As a consequence, the character name "Scrooge" became permanently attached to my profile. Overnight, my fame eclipsed every other student on campus, leading many to recognize me solely as "Scrooge". Some later even presumed it to be my given name.

The significance of Eastern Junior was multi-fold and extended beyond this event. Mr. Conliffe, an authoritative figure customarily donning a tie and a crisp white short-sleeved shirt, was a stern disciplinarian with a quick belt. His imposing presence struck fear in our hearts, his penetrating stare and scrutinizing gaze often steering our actions. Even his daughter Eleanor, a classmate, was not immune to his firm hand. His austere demeanor served as a stark warning to all.

However, underneath this stern exterior was a man possessed of an uncanny vision. He perceived the unique potential of our Class 4. With a drive to ensure our academic triumph beyond the confines of the imminent secondary education, he urged us to consider enrolling in private high schools like St. John's, St. Augustine's, and **The** Government High School. These institutions, unlike Eastern Senior School, required success in an entrance exam. As such, Mr. Conliffe viewed it as his sacred mission to prepare us for the future national leadership roles he envisioned for us.

He went above and beyond, committing to afternoon and weekend classes focusing primarily on English and Mathematics - the essential components of the entrance exams. In these extra tutorials, we came to know a man whose heart for young people and their deserved success seemed boundless. He was saturated with a generous spirit that contradicted his otherwise unfriendly appearance. The distinction of attending a "High School" held a certain prestige, possibly due to the assumption of its superior academic standards.

Even amongst private schools, St. Augustine's College (SAC) stood out. With a rigorous curriculum delivered by highly qualified educators, an extended school day, and an emphasis on sports and religious teachings, SAC seemed like the perfect fit for me.

Rewinding a few years, I remember the desolate feeling about leaving Roses, Long Island, that January 1961, morning. It was an event, in retrospect, that altered my trajectory forever. Presciently, Grandma and Dad discerned that the educational prospects I needed could not be provided in a Long Island all-age school. The decision to attend Eastern Junior and subsequently SAC attested to that.

Sharing the school premises with extraordinary talents like twins Arthur and Otto Fountain, successful entrepreneurs, as well as other eminent personalities such as Colleen Colebrook, Richard Marshall, Thelma Ferguson, Eddie Smith, Audley (Fred) Mitchell, and Walter Hanchell, among others, sparked in me an urge to push the boundaries of my potential.

Mr. Conliffe, with his visionary insight, perceived that the customary progression from a primary school like ours to an attached secondary school would fail to fully unearth our latent talents. He was adamant that we sit for the entrance exams of ***all*** the notable private schools. But my mind was steadfastly fixated on one ONLY — SAC.

His genius lay in his ability to comprehend what we needed to be prepared for the entrance exams. He didn't just coach us—he examined the minutiae of the different exams by communicating with the various private school principals to understand its structure. Although college was never explicitly discussed as our ultimate destination, I'm certain he understood that a private high school 'guaranteed' for us a much clearer path towards higher education than a public one would.

A pivotal moment arrived one bright Saturday morning in May 1964 when I, along with twelve other students, sat the SAC entrance exam. Little did we know then how much this moment would come to shape our futures.

Chapter Nine

Big Red Machine (SAC)

My religious foundations were deeply anchored in Anglicanism, taking root at St. Margaret's Church on Kemp Road. From a tender age, I formed close relationships with revered figures such as Father Michael Eldon, who later ascended to the bishopric, the late Father Collingwood Cooper, and the late Bishop Donald Knowles, who shared a deep friendship with my mother. Yet, it was only one Catholic priest that I knew as a youngster - Father Thomas LaVerge, who pastored St. Bede's in my neighborhood.

In the humble confines of St. Augustine's College's compact classroom that fateful Saturday morning, Father Bonaventure Dean spoke words of wisdom that would outline the pathways of my life. He was an imposing figure, striding like a majestic peacock through the narrow classroom lined with orderly desks. His admonition resounded: "You must write neatly and legibly." The term 'legibly' initially seemed arcane to me, but his meaning was clear. His grandeur was evident in his towering posture, attired in a pristine, flowing cassock. He paced the room with an air of unassailable authority, exuding a magnetic presence that temporarily quelled my examination jitters.

He was the proctor who presided over the entrance examination. His charisma was otherworldly, amalgamating a unique blend of intelligence, forthrightness, and brilliance, alongside an air of clear and commanding presence, the likes of which I had never witnessed before. His piercing gaze seemed to bore right into my soul, his large, black-framed glasses acting as the lens to scrutinize my character.

"On this," he instructed, holding aloft a lined, white sheet of paper, "you must tell us why you want to come to St. Augustine's." His words accompanied the distribution of the examination papers and culminated in a solemn proclamation. "I will tell you when to put your pens down," he concluded.

Breaking the news to my mother that I wished to sit the SAC examination evoked a concoction of awe and anxiety within her. Pride filled her heart at the prospect that her eldest offspring's intellect was being recognized by a private institution, but it was simultaneously tinged with worry about the financial toll it would inflict. SAC was far from an affordable institution; its fees alone seemed insurmountable, given our limited means. This notwithstanding, I vividly recalled her discussing it with Dad, , with the conversation concluding on a hopeful note of, "We'll see how it goes."

The parental instinct to secure the best future for one's offspring is as natural as the sunrise. Despite adversities – whether financial, geographical, or otherwise – parents contrive creative solutions to pave the path for their children's success.

The examination followed the lines of Mr. Conliffe's guidance, consisting of two parts: mathematics and an essay. After tackling the math section with ease and adhering religiously to Mr. Conliffe's advice for the essay, I found myself securing the second-highest score among all participants that year, bested only by a Jamaican student who lived in Nassau.

Despite my parents' steady employment, their income was hardly affluent, especially considering the hefty SAC school fees. Our humble abode was nestled in the less privileged sector of New Providence – Kemp Road. Yet, I held a steadfast belief that I would walk the hallowed halls of SAC. And what a journey it unfolded to be!

Entering SAC was like diving into a whirlpool of exhilarating adventures. The school's unique traits only enhanced its allure. Its long distance from home, the all-male student body, the onerous weekday schedule stretching from 8 am to 8 pm, the monochromatic gray uniforms that were reminiscent of a prison, and the institution's supervision by monks — were features that could have been daunting, but instead, amplified my attraction to the school.

The perception of SAC as an esteemed establishment resonated with my parents as well. Their pride was palpable when I broke the news of my successful exam, igniting a desire to pursue my education there. The day we met with Father Burton Blooms, SAC's Principal, in his quaint office, is still stamped in my memory. His admiration of my exam score was evident, and his insistence that my parents find the means to nurture my potential played a pivotal role in cementing my place in SAC the following September. Post-meeting, I discerned a new twinkle of joy in my parents' eyes, their eldest son now the beacon of their dreams.

My achievement wasn't personal. Indeed, it was a milestone for my entire family and the Kemp Road community. Attendance at a private high school was a seldom-treaded path, and I was the pioneer in my maternal and paternal families to embark on this journey. This feat, previously unimaginable due to the astronomical costs and a lack of exposure, was made possible through the unwavering vision, inspiration, and perseverance of my mentor, Dawson Conliffe.

September 1964, marked my grand entrance into SAC, where I was reunited with the iconic figure of my admission exam, Father Bonaventure, the Dean of Students. His stunning linguistic command and an air of confidence reignited my aspiration to emulate his persona.

Life at SAC wasn't all rosy. The 'rod of correction', a 30" x 3" razor strap wielded by Father Bonaventure, was an occasional painful reminder of the rigorous discipline expected of us. Despite the occasional harsh encounter with the 'rod', Father Bonaventure, affectionately known as 'BON', along with Mr. Leviticus 'Lou' Adderley, Father Burton Blooms, Anthony Kimber, Father Leander Thompson, and Educar the Janitor, left indelible imprints on our lives.

My zeal for involvement propelled me to participate in a gamut of activities. From track and field to basketball and softball, I dabbled in them all. My true calling, though, was discovered early on – singing, a craft to which I dedicated four memorable years in the school's choir, aptly named the Chorus, under the tutelage of Father Bartholomew Sayles, or "Fr. Tuck".

The Chorus wasn't solely a platform for vocal talents but also a stage for theatrical brilliance. Along with Father Aaron Kraft ("Jerry"), Father Bartholomew produced two captivating stage productions each academic year. Performances like The Batsman Bride and My Fair Lady were among the many productions in which I played significant roles.

However, my commitment to the Chorus was not without conflict. Tuck's strict insistence on an exclusive commitment to this activity curtailed my sporting aspirations and that of many other students. After four long years, I mustered the courage to confront him with an ultimatum: either allow me to play Volleyball, or I will leave the Chorus. He retaliated with threats of expulsion from school, but I stood my ground, which was eventually supported by Principal Father Bonaventure, who knew my worth and contribution to SAC.

Even today, I feel the sting of being robbed of potential athletic glory due to his inflexible rule. I knew I could have excelled as a multi-talented athlete and performer, but was deterred by his inane restrictions. Despite numerous attempts by coaches such as Father Alvin, who praised my athletic prowess, they all failed to convince him. Consequently, I was never able to break free from the chorus's restrictive cocoon.

Bartholomew, was a daunting figure, with a volatile temper that many, I suspect, were hesitant to cross. He resisted losing me from the Chorus because male involvement was low, largely due to his absurd regulations. Additionally, the biannual plays were immensely popular, playing to standing-room-only crowds over consecutive weekends. I could, therefore, understand why he feared my departure.

My mother took immense pride in my involvement with the Chorus, as she herself was a lead singer in St. Margaret's Church choir. This association with the choral and theatrical world not only made me a familiar face within SAC but also laid the groundwork for my future public presentation endeavors. The discipline, rigorous training, and refinement of my voice through my choral career became invaluable assets, honing my oratorical delivery and equipping me with the skills necessary for effective public presentations.

The turning point of my school life, however, arrived in my third year, or Grade 10, when Father Bonaventure appointed me and two others as the official scorers for the annual Inter-House Track & Field meet. This honor marked my ascension as a student leader, as I was, subsequently, chosen by the administration to lead various student body activities. The respect I gained from my peers through these roles led to a momentous surprise in March, 1968, a day that still gleams brightly in my memory.

Girls, Girls

The autumnal canvas of SAC's campus underwent a metamorphosis in 1967, at the commencement of my fourth academic year. An unprecedented amalgamation took place; the once all-female Xavier's College was absorbed by the historically all-male SAC. The underlying motivation for such a monumental decision, I reasoned, must have been well-thought-out and logical. A prime incentive cannot be divorced from financial considerations. Economically, it was pragmatic to consolidate two institutions sharing the same educational objective. Yet, I could not help but ponder if the drive for monetary efficiency may have eclipsed other intelligent reasons that warranted maintaining separate gender-centric establishments. Indeed, the foundational philosophy behind the inception of both institutions was rooted in the conviction that Bahamian boys and girls required divergent environments to flourish, to maximize their latent potential. This premise was validated by their alumni who embodied well-rounded personalities and outstanding educational accomplishments, a testament that stands unassailably true.

Even today, the debate surrounding the merits of single-gender schools reverberates through the corridors of academia. I find myself firmly anchored in the camp advocating its benefits for a ***certain*** cohort of students. The assertion that one academic solution or pedagogical model fits all is, in my opinion, inherently flawed. At its core, an educational system should serve one single purpose: the aspirations of its students. It must be sensitive to the diverse palate of its clientele, each arriving with unique needs, ambitions, and prerequisites. Some students thrive in a rigid, disciplined environment, simulating a military school ethos, while others flourish under the nurturing, homely supervision that a boarding environment provides. Then there are the outliers, those self-driven individuals who navigate life with minimal external supervision. They are autonomous, disciplined, driven, and in possession of a clear vision of their goals and ambitions, possessing the tenacity to pursue them with little adult intervention.

Some students lean towards a more academic trajectory, while others gravitate towards hands-on learning experiences. I've encountered parents who opted for single-gender education out of concern that adolescent hormonal surges might lead their child to ill-considered actions, or perhaps because they believed their child would fare better learning among peers of the same sex. Some wished to shield an introverted child from potential distractions and bullying that could arise from interaction with the opposite sex. For such students, the presence of contemporaries of the opposite gender could be an unwelcome hindrance to their life objectives. Regardless of the motivation or selection, the education system should offer a variety of options to individual preferences.

Today's world, however, contrasts starkly with the past, with parents exercising increased control over their children's education, often veering towards home-based or home-schooling options. Decades of global research, dating back to 1974, has thrown light on the powerful benefits that a single-sex educational environment can offer certain students. A 2015 publication titled 'About Education' by Dr. Blythe Grossberg, a noted American expert on private education with decades of experience working with students, parents, and administrators at private schools in New York City, underscores the potential advantages of single-sex schools. She highlights a few key characteristics that typify such institutions, namely:

a. A less stressful environment for males; and

b. A tailored curriculum

Dr. Grossberg suggests that the curriculum in single-sex schools can be designed specifically for the gender of the students, enabling teachers to structure classes that truly resonate with the learners. She asserts that in boys' schools, teachers can delve into topics that speak to boys' interests and concerns. For instance, a study of Hamlet could focus on a boy's coming-of-age and father-son relationships. In girls' schools, the curriculum can offer a focus on literature featuring robust female protagonists such as Jane Eyre or The House of Mirth, addressing prevailing societal attitudes towards women. While these themes can indeed find their place in co-educational schools, their exploration can be deeper, more nuanced, and concentrated in single-sex environments.

Dr. Grossberg's insights dovetail with numerous other studies I've encountered, which highlight that boys and girls educated in single-sex settings often develop increased self-confidence. It's critical to underscore, however, that this model is optimally suited for a particular subset of students.[1]

Student Council Election

The tangible implementation of the unification policy resulted in a distinct divide between the genders. Even though cohabitating on the same grounds, girls were primarily stationed at the lower campus. They were integrated with the boys in some lessons, while the boys dominated the classes at the upper campus. Initially, the introduction of girls proved somewhat uncomfortable, yet this unease soon dissipated and became a mere afterthought. Inevitably, the innate attraction between the genders blossomed into clandestine romances, some discreet, others more conspicuous.

The merger also resulted in the restructuring of the student council with the introduction of two vice presidents, one for each gender. Elections for the senior-year council were held in the spring of our fourth year, set into motion by a preceding nomination day.

In April 1968, I was chosen by the administration to oversee the nomination process. Entrusted with the role by the Dean of Students, Mr.

Nunez, I was tasked to organize a group of students to collect and calculate nomination ballots from various homerooms.

"Hey, Scrooge, you see what's happening?" Preston Albury, a close friend, and a fellow fourth-year student, nicknamed "Slinger", blurted out as we began tallying the votes. As a member of the team I supervised, Slinger was a quick learner. "You're being nominated for both President *and* Vice President," he excitedly revealed. I was taken aback, the magnitude of this revelation not truly sinking in since I was immersed in the duty Mr. Nunez had assigned me. However, as we tabulated the votes, certain names were clear favorites for the council's leadership. As Slinger had observed, mine was among them.

By the close of the day, I had secured a clear majority of votes for the position of Boys' Vice President, surpassing my closest rival, Don Taylor, and had garnered the second-highest votes for President. No doubt, my previous assignments around campus held a positive impression in the hearts and minds of many students, who, obviously, held my demonstrated capabilities in respected esteem.

Before these events, I had never been a member of the student council. The administration alone executed the council's selection process, with criteria unknown to the wider student population. I couldn't pinpoint any particular reason for my emergence as a male student leader, aside from the fact that I regularly starred in drama productions, was a starter on the senior boy's volleyball team, was a skilled organizer, patriotic to SAC's ideals, frequently selected by the administration for special tasks around the campus, and was, overall, quite a well-liked student. Nonetheless, there I was, leading the roster of nominated candidates for Boys' Vice President. A friend, Patrick Cash, was the undeniable first choice for the office of President. The outcome of the contest for Boys' Vice President, however, was hardly a surprise, with Don losing to me by a ratio of 3 to 1.

Don was an exceptional student and friend, known for his gentle demeanor and steadfast commitment to hard work, diligence, and conscientiousness. The student council elections were held just weeks after the PLP's triumphant general election victory on April 10th, 1968. However, the political climate in The Bahamas over the previous year and a half induced anxiety among some Bahamians. This 1968 decisive victory surpassed the marginal majority the party had won on January 10th, 1967. The period following gave rise to an intoxicating sense of euphoria throughout the country. We, students, were swept up in this tide of joy, pride, and boundless optimism. However, not all Bahamians shared in this ecstasy. Some reacted with visceral indignation at the prospect of a black majority seizing the reins of the political power. Fearful declarations of never consenting to live under a black administration reverberated in some quarters, leading to an exodus of many families from The Bahamas to places as far-flung as the United States, Canada, Europe, and Australia.

During this life-changing era, SAC's convocations were dominated by stirring displays of nationalistic rhetoric, including passionate speeches by students like Anthony Johnson and Patrick Cash, both deceased, articulating the hopes of the young generation of Bahamians. The nation was enthralled by an unprecedented sense of possibility, empowerment, and hope - a sensation that was new to my limited 16 years on this earth.

This sense of possibility - that we were on the precipice of a vibrant, prosperous future - was pervasive, seeping into many homes and neighborhoods. The phrase 'Building The Bahamas' assumed profound significance, symbolizing the creation of a modern society where all Bahamians, particularly those of black heritage, could fulfill their potential.

Before that momentous January 10th, 1967, the prospects for social, economic, or political advancement for black Bahamians were severely curtailed. However, the elections of 1967 and 1968 dramatically altered this narrative, ushering in an historic era of change.

A figure of pivotal influence in my young life during this time was Father Bonaventure Dean, who assumed the role of SAC's Principal in 1967. To impressionable youths like myself, he was a venerated hero. His passionate statements in the aftermath of Premier Lynden Pindling's election left no doubt about his ardent hope for a brighter future for all Bahamians. He even served as one of Mr. Pindling's closest advisors at one point.

On nomination day, I was astounded by the high regard in which my peers held me. From the day I first stepped into SAC, the Monks ingrained in us the belief that anything was achievable with hard work. Their point was that it wasn't because there was something extraordinary about us, but rather because there ***was*** something exceptional within us. This mindset, this belief in our innate worth and potential seeped into the core of our being, eventually shaping the trajectory of our lives.

Indeed, my time at SAC had an overpowering impact on me, so much so that I later coined the saying: "There are two kinds of people in the world: Those who went to SAC, and those who wished they did." This saying elicited varied reactions, from admiration and amusement to accusations of arrogance and insolence. I intended to not just laud the extraordinary institution that had profoundly influenced me and countless others but to highlight its amazing blend of academic, athletic, cultural, and spiritual education. It captured the essence of excellence the Monks envisioned for us.

The five years I spent at SAC molded my worldview, instilled in me a strong sense of identity, and charted the course of my reality, which became the springboard from which I launched myself into the world.

The year 1968 was a banner year for me on a personal level. Not only did I triumph in the Student Council election, but also clinched one of the leading roles in the spring production of 'My Fair Lady,' where I portrayed Alfred Doolittle.

Taking on the role of Doolittle was no small task. It required long hours of rehearsal, mastering the intricacies of an English accent, quite a feat for a Bahamian teenager. But the satisfaction I derived from that experience was unparalleled.

Moreover, working alongside a dedicated cast and crew was hugely beneficial. I learned the value of collaboration and teamwork, and how different perspectives and talents could coalesce to create something greater than the sum of its parts. The camaraderie, the shared passion, and the adrenaline of opening night - were the moments that brought us together, and galvanized into a coherent, dynamic troupe.

The play was a resounding success. Playing to packed houses and standing ovations at each performance, we basked in the glow of praise and admiration from peers, faculty, and community members alike. Even the "Bon", ever the stern taskmaster, commended us on our performance, a rare and cherished accolade.

But 1968 was not merely about personal accomplishments. It was also about the continued evolution of my beloved Bahamas, as it traversed the aftermath of a political sea change. There was a newfound sense of progress and unity. It was as if the entire nation had taken a collective breath and, for the first time in our history, dared to dream.

And dream we did: of a country where everyone, regardless of race, social status, or background, could thrive; of a future where children and grandchildren could stand tall, proud of their heritage, confident in their potential, and that of a country that would not only survive but prosper in the 21st century.

Those dreams are still alive today, though the road has not always been smooth, and the journey is far from over. There have been setbacks, disappointments, and even heartbreaks. But the spirit of The Bahamas, the unyeilding resilience that inaugurated that historic victory in 1967, remains unbroken.

As I look back on that pivotal year, I am filled with a profound sense of gratitude; for the opportunities that came my way; the lessons learned; the friendships forged; and the chance to be a part of something greater than myself.

1968 was, indeed, a banner year. But it was just the beginning of a journey that continues to this day, as I strive to honor the lessons and values instilled in me by my SAC experience and the life-changing events that shaped my beloved Bahamas. I am forever indebted to those experiences, which serve as a constant reminder to never stop striving, never stop dreaming, and never stop believing in the potential of The Bahamas.

---

1. Blythe Grossberg, Updated on October 14, 2019: Advantages of Single-Sex Schools: ThoughtCo

1st Year at SAC - 1965

Group 11, Form 1

Jeffrey with friend, Gregory Lampkin

Member, SAC Senior Boys Volleyball Team

Chapter Ten

College Years

"**You *are going* to** college" was a constant refrain endlessly repeated from the moment I crossed the threshold of SAC in the autumn of 1964. The vision of a college education was a distant and near-impossible specter for my parents. But for my classmates and me, it morphed into a fervent aspiration. It was not a question of 'if', but rather 'where'. By the time we entered Third Form (Grade 10), SAC began to sculpt us intensively for that impending future.

Each May, we eagerly awaited one of the many "convocations" - presentations by SAC alumni who were basking in the glory of college life. They graced the campus annually, sharing their collegiate experiences with us. Their narratives did not always paint the picturesque tableau of campus life that we envisioned. Instead, their accounts served to induce both a healthy fear and a deep respect for the tertiary educational experience, though tinged with exhilarating anticipation.

Like many before us, embarking on a university journey meant leaving the safety of home for an extended period. As the idea of attending SAC had once ignited a fear within me, the thought of college did the same. The prohibitive cost of education, coupled with my apprehension about handling the academic rigor—especially since I had never fully lived up to my academic potential -- —casted an ominous shadow over my aspirations. I worried about the strain a college education would impose on my mother's finances. Though St. Gregory's yearly fees for tuition, room, and board amounted to $1,500, it was a sum my family could hardly afford.

Financial support from my father was a non-option. His earning potential was a mere whisper against the loud echo of my mother's income, despite his superior qualifications. Though a housekeeper, she had numerous employments in affluent white households, the longest of which was the Normans. This wealthy retired New York couple had been her employers for many years. Unbeknownst to me at the time, they funded my entire college education, their affection for me being as profound as that for my mother. Despite her frequent encouragement to connect with them, I rarely ever did.

Quite frankly, I doubted my readiness and ability to overcome the complexities of college. My study habits left much to be desired, primarily due to an embarrassing shortfall in discipline and time management. The prospect of flunking out was horrifying. The shame it would bring to my family and the burden it would pose to my mother and the magnanimous Normans were unbearable. Thus, I was compelled by the necessity to step up to the challenge, project confidence, and address the deficiency in my study habits that plagued my high school years.

On August 24th, 1969, I, along with ten other SAC graduates and a few parents/chaperones, left the shores of The Bahamas for St. Gregory's College, known as St. Greg's, in Shawnee, Oklahoma, marking another pivotal step in the amazing trek that commenced five years earlier at SAC. It was an incredibly rewarding expedition for me and the twenty-five other SAC and Aquinas College graduates whom Fr. Alvin Fong Ben, the Vice Principal and Senior Class Moderator of SAC, had arranged to enroll at St. Greg's.

St. Gregory's College

St. Greg's, a Junior college, sat nestled among the cow-grazed farmlands of Shawnee, thirty-eight miles south of Oklahoma City and twenty-two miles north of Norman, home to the University of Oklahoma and the renowned Oklahoma Sooners. Operated by the monks of St. Gregory's Abbey, a Benedictine monastery formerly affiliated with St. John's ArchAbbey in Collegeville, Minnesota, St. Greg's held deep ties with some of the monks at SAC. Many were once classmates with the monks of St. Greg's. Leveraging this connection, St. Greg's successfully attracted a significant number of students from The Bahamas.

In hindsight, this served as an ideal stepping stone for most of us. The intimidating nature of larger colleges and universities, with student populations in the tens of thousands, would have posed a daunting challenge for sheltered eighteen-year-olds from the Bahamas in the 60's. St. Greg's, with its intimate environment, became a safe haven for us. The monks' familiarity with The Bahamas and their constant yet subtle oversight fostered a familial atmosphere that made the transition from home to college smoother. I left the Bahamas without a definite career path in mind, but the submerged interest in the priesthood continued to lurk within me. My upbringing in Kemp Road was sprinkled with visions of becoming a preacher, where I was captivated by religious ministers of all denominations, be they Anglican, Catholic, or Protestant.

At St. Greg's, I began to truly contemplate this calling. This question simmered just beneath the surface of my consciousness, occasionally stirred with greater intensity. Once I enrolled at St. Greg's, I plunged headfirst into campus life, joining the school choir, acting as a cantor at Sunday masses, participating in the drama club, The Masquers, and refereeing intramural sporting competitions. Being a pre-drama major, I immersed myself in all theatrical activities, thus exposing me to all facets of the dramatic arts.

Indeed, my first semester there wasn't much different than high school, save for the ache of homesickness. Though the pace and intensity of work were noticeably higher than in high school, it was not as overwhelming as I had feared. As I mentioned before, my struggle was not due to a lack of potential, but rather the absence of effective study and time management habits. Initially, I didn't seize the opportunity that St. Greg's presented to overcome this deficiency. The dizzying social whirl of risk-taking and exposure, which were held at bay during high school, added another layer to my struggle.

As I journeyed through my two years there, a desire grew within me to attend a school where students shared my appearance, thoughts, and actions. St. Greg's student body was composed of only ten percent black students, the majority of whom were Bahamians. Therefore, during my sophomore year, I began searching for a campus with a larger black student population. Satisfying this desire was Xavier University of the South in New Orleans, Louisiana, where several Bahamians had previously attended. Being a predominantly black institution, it perfectly fitted my criterion, and the decision to transfer there was an easy one.

In September 1971, I, along with a few fellow students enrolled at Xavier University.

However, the transition to Xavier did not come without its costs. I hadn't fully comprehended the implications of the shift. The transfer resulted in the loss of twenty-four credit hours, essentially a semester and a half of college work, necessitating an additional semester to complete my bachelor's degree.

While St. Greg's did pose its fair share of academic hurdles, Xavier proved to be an entirely different ballgame. From the moment I set foot on the campus, I felt an invigorating rush of vitality. Both socially and academically, I came into my own at Xavier. As the saying goes, I truly found my groove.

During my time at Xavier, I was exposed to an enriching kaleidoscope of thoughts, ideas, and experiences. Every interaction, every lecture, every casual conversation in the university's hallways contributed to my evolution. I absorbed lessons not just from textbooks, but from life itself.

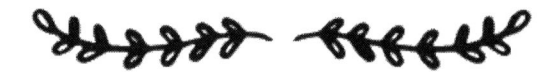

Xavier U

In many ways, Xavier presented a fertile landscape for my growth and development. The vibrant, multicultural atmosphere ignited my intellectual curiosity, fostering a profound shift in my academic trajectory. It was not only about adopting better study habits but also about cultivating an enriched perspective on life and my role within it.

The dynamic city of New Orleans mirrored The Bahamas, my home. Its majority black populace, radiating an infectious warmth and amiability, was reminiscent of my people. They shared my sensitivities, my humor, and my struggle. Their gregarious nature exceeded that which I had encountered in Shawnee. In this corner of Louisiana, I felt at ease, a sense of belonging that permeated every aspect of my life.

Though I was a student at Xavier, circumstances required me to reside in the verdant grounds of Loyola University of the South, just a short, scenic 15-minute bus journey away. Loyola's appendage, 'of the South', was not merely for geographical reference, but rather to distinguish it from its sister institutions scattered across the country, like the esteemed Loyola Marymount University in California, Loyola of Maryland, and Loyola of Illinois. All these prestigious establishments fell under the broad jurisdiction of the Catholic Jesuit Order. An unexpected housing crisis at Xavier required several students, including myself and my roommate Tyrone, to find a home in Loyola. Our temporary abode was on Ferret Street, directly across the grandeur of Tulane University. Compared to Xavier, Loyola's dormitory facilities were a marked improvement, a blend of comfort and refinement.

My spirit truly awakened in New Orleans, a city that nurtured deep friendships which has stood the test of time. Treasured among the many lasting relationships that I formed were those with Cephas Shepard, Barry Bonner, Clarence Lott, Hercules Granger, Gregg Pappion, Frank Taylor, Delores Thibodeaux, Ras Cloud Prejean, Sharon Taylor, and countless others. Cephas, Frank, Barry, and Hercules transcended the ordinary definition of friendship, becoming brothers bound not by blood but by shared experiences and aspirations. My bond with Cephas was underscored by fascinating similarities: our birthdays were only three days apart, and both of us had affections for a girl named Karen. A personal crisis involving my mother in 1971 led me to spend an unforgettable Christmas holiday with Cephas' family in Mobile, Alabama. Being the

Yuletide season, it was tinged with the melancholy of missing family and the rhythmic, hypnotic beat of junkanoo, yet filled with memories forged in Mobile that ultimately strengthened my bond with Cephas and his kin.

Upon my arrival in New Orleans, I purchased a used 1963 Cadillac, a mechanical beast we affectionately christened "the Kitten." For the following two years, this trusted vehicle ferried me and my friends, most of whom hailed from Mobile, back and forth virtually every weekend. At Xavier, my circle expanded to include remarkable Professors like Mr. Parchman, Dr. Jay Springman, and the University's pioneering black President, Dr. Norman Francis.

An advantageous consortium arrangement existed between Xavier and three New Orleans colleges: Loyola, Tulane, and the all-female Dominican College. It allowed students, officially enrolled in one of these schools, to take credit courses at the other campuses, as long as the majority of their coursework was completed at their home campus. This was particularly appealing to me since my passion lay in communications. Loyola was renowned for its distinguished communications programs in the southeastern region, a discipline unfortunately lacking at Xavier. The facilities were state-of-the-art, complete with the city's leading radio and television stations, Channels 4 Radio and Television, both CBS affiliates.

Because of its size, my options in the small Drama/Journalism Department at Xavier were limited in scope. However, the demands of the courses kept us engaged with a rigorously active schedule. Consequently, I was engrossed in every facet of stage productions - from playing leading or supporting roles to directing, producing, and managing the intricacies of set design, costume, or lighting. The whirlwind of parallel productions often required drama majors to juggle multiple roles across different shows, turning my major into a demanding, yet gratifying, whirligig.

Journalism, my minor, complemented my major perfectly. It allowed me to write, produce, and edit stories for the campus newspaper, the Herald. My constant involvement and dedication eventually earned me the position of Associate Editor. The culmination of my studies required the completion of a department-approved project in my chosen discipline. I opted to direct two three-act productions, one each for theater and television. Additionally, the project further included scripting, producing, and directing several other television shows at Loyola. In a bid to broaden my radio experience, I once sought employment at Loyola's campus station. Although my application went unanswered, it did little to diminish my enthusiasm.

Throughout this exhaustive period of academic and creative involvement, I consistently maintained a superior grade point average above 3.0, a significant leap from my disappointing performance at St. Greg's.

On a more personal front, Xavier marked a pivotal moment in my life. There I was, as we phrased it then, "turned on" to drugs. From the first encounter with marijuana, my world morphed dramatically, and my consciousness expanded in unimaginable ways.

As a person naturally inclined towards introspection and inquiry, I was an ideal candidate for the mind-augmenting effects of marijuana. Although only vaguely apparent at the time, I later realized that my disposition was attuned to a contemplative life, one deeply immersed in the art and science of meditation, which eventually became my primary spiritual practice. The use of marijuana served as a catalyst, igniting this latent propensity for contemplation to the forefront of my experience.

During many of my "high" periods, I gleaned profound insights into a multitude of issues and facets of life, my homeland, and the world at large. Oddly, despite never developing concrete study habits in college, it was at Xavier that my grades soared consistently above a 3.0 average. Looming always in my consciousness, though, was the knowledge that college was but a hiatus, a brief interlude between student life and full-time employment. I understood that after this sojourn, employment waited.

In the fall of 1973, I completed my studies, choosing not to return for the graduation ceremony in May 1974, citing the uncertainty of travel due to the ongoing oil crisis. Thankfully, the Academic Dean understood and exempted me from participating. Through the crucible of those grueling years, I emerged not just with a degree in hand, but with a more holistic understanding of myself and the world. I was no longer the timid freshman who stepped onto the campus of St. Greg's in 1969. I had become a confident young man ready to meet the world head-on, with a firm belief in my capabilities and a resolute commitment to my dreams.

The college memories remain imprinted in my heart, serving as poignant reminders of the journey that brought me to where I am today. Indeed, the experience of tertiary education shaped my life in ways I could never have foreseen. It remains a testament to the fortifying power of academic training and the enduring resilience of the human spirit.

St. Gregory's College
1971

St. Gregory's College, Student, 1971

St. Gregory's College
Black Students Association, 1971

Xavier University
1972

Xavier Student ID Card

Xavier Graduation Photo

SELF-DISCOVERY

Chapter Eleven

Work Life

Although my mother never directly stated it, there existed, nevertheless, an unspoken understanding that the moment I reached employable age, my school summer breaks would be occupied with work. This self-imposed expectation steered me down paths of various experiences, beginning as a novice helper at the City Market Food Store on Frederick Street, Nassau, to warehouse assistant at Pepsi Cola, where I served under the stern management of the late Philip Pinder, a former Member of Parliament.

From Pepsi, I moved to the Bahamian Club Restaurant on West Bay Street, then as a summer intern at the Bahamas Customs Department, and eventually managing various Bethell-Robertson bars, with intermittent stints in the construction trade. It was at Customs where I first met the Hon. Frank Watson who, at that time, was the Deputy Comptroller, and eventually rose to become the Comptroller. To my surprise, I discovered that we were distantly related on my paternal grandmother's side. Our shared ancestry originated from our great-grandparents - my great-grandmother, Margaret Watson was a sibling (I was told) of Frank's great-grandfather. To this day, Frank affectionately refers to me as "cuz".

Those summer exploits served as a substructure of my professional ethos, grounding me with a robust work ethic that continues to shape my life, fostering an intense awareness of responsibility and accountability, and developing a fierce commitment to teamwork. Although my Customs supervisor, the late Rev. Garth Greene, was of superior intellect and intuition, it was Robert "Bob" Dames at City Market who truly mentored me. Despite his paucity of formal academic qualifications, Bob was immensely attentive, patient, and compassionate, a stark contrast to the icy demeanor I encountered in Philip Pinder. The only reason I worked at Pepsi was likely due to my mother's employment by Pepsi's General Manager, Mr. Maura, a US citizen whom Pinder had brought to The Bahamas, leveraging his expansive managerial expertise with Pepsi franchises in the United States.

Despite the frosty dynamics of our relationship, I admired and respected Mr. Pinder's incisive business acumen. He possessed invaluable business insights, from which one could benefit hugely once one was able to overlook his challenging persona and attitude. Much as journalists possess a 'nose for news,' he had a distinctive knack for identifying lucrative business opportunities well before others could. I was informed that during his campaigning as a PLP candidate for the Delaporte constituency, he would request the use of a householders' bathroom, not for relief, but to conduct impromptu market research. This unconventional approach laid the foundation for his future business strategies.

Another interesting experience from which I gained valued life lessons was the cummer management of the bars. I, along with my Fountain brothers, took turns substituting for vacationing bartenders. The experiences were unequaled for the depth of perception that we observed in the minds of ordinary citizens who, though of the lower socio-economic profile, possessed uncanny wisdom of the subtle features of life from the bottom, as it were. There, additionally, were genuine friendships that have withstood the test of time, including those with the regular patrons who became unexpected mentors. Among them was Henry Wemyss, a former police officer, who continues to be a cherished friend to this day.

Upon graduation from Xavier in December 1973, Daddy Bert offered me a permanent position as a bartender, but my sights were set on broader horizons. With determination in my heart, I immediately applied for a news reporter position at ZNS, where I was already acquainted with Mr. Walter Wisdom, ZNS's General Manager. During our conversation about a potential permanent role, he inquired about my previous summer with them, which left him and me perplexed.

"I didn't work here for the summer, Sir," I clarified, as a wave of incredulity washed over his face. Our confusion was mutual. Apparently, he had directed that I be hired for the summer, a command that had somehow slipped through the bureaucratic maze at ZNS, a subsidiary of

The Bahamas Civil Service, where dysfunction and incompetence were, unfortunately, not uncommon.

Undeterred by this oversight, he made it his personal mission that I join the ZNS family. Thus, on February 18th, 1974, my journalistic voyage began as a Cub Reporter with the national radio station, fulfilling a long-held aspiration. The allure of broadcasting had always captivated me. My father, a voracious consumer of current affairs, instilled within me a deep respect for the news. His daily ritual of reading the newspaper from cover to cover, coupled with the sacred silence in our home during radio newscasts, engendered a deep reverence for the news.

This veneration for the news was not limited to us but seemed to dominate most Bahamian homes. Newscasts were perceived as cannons of truth, with listeners often considering their content as irrefutable fact. Even today, many hold this belief. That's why, when I later became a Media personality, I prioritized vigorous fact-checking to ensure that my shows presented accurate and verifiable information, whether from me, a guest, or a caller. I considered it my patriotic duty to maintain this standard of integrity, realizing that Bahamians often endowed the media with unwavering trust, occasionally more than it deserved. It was evident that discerning fact from opinion or conjecture proved challenging for some.

However, my tenure at ZNS was short-lived, despite the sincere entreaties from several well-meaning managers. As it turned out, destiny had charted a different course for my career, a path that awaited me with the promise of exciting adventures and invaluable lessons.

Teaching at SAC

"Jeff?" The question hung in the air like a soft-spoken melody, interrupting my frantic evening of news preparation. As a recent assignee to the 10 p.m. news slot, I was still learning these uncertain waters, their depths stirred by my own anxiety and determined pursuit of excellence.

"This is Jeff Lloyd speaking," I responded, using the radio pseudonym that had, over time, gained a touch of prestige. My moniker was buoyed by the established fame of ZNS's beloved DJ Jeff Scavella, making it easier for another 'Jeff' to find a foothold in people's memory.

The voice continued; its familiarity unraveling in the quiet hum of the late-night office. "This is Mr. Adderley. How are you?" Recognition clicked into place, but the unexpected call left me startled.

"I'm okay, Sir. Is everything alright?" I ventured, my tone echoing the mild surprise and curiosity stirred by this sudden interaction. Leviticus "Lou" Adderley, my former Math and PE teacher, was then the Principal at my alma mater, SAC.

The rhythm of my ZNS job, dictated by a split-shift system, had me anchored at the station during odd hours. I split my time between stints from 10 a.m. to 2 p.m., and then again from 6 p.m. to 10:30 p.m. That night, I was wrapping up another such day.

"I'm looking for an English teacher. Could you help me?" The unforeseen proposition perfumed the night, a tune sweeter than the most harmonious choir of angels, singing "Glory, Halleluia!!" directly into my awestruck ears.

"Would you be able to take a teaching position at SAC this September? The English teacher just quit." He added, as if amplifying the divine chorus resonating in my ears.

The notion of becoming a teacher at SAC rendered me momentarily speechless. If ever a dream job existed - not that I had consciously envisioned teaching - it would have been at this institution, my cherished alma mater, the one place where my life had taken a meteoric flight.

My mother later revealed that she had given Mr. Adderley my work contact earlier that evening. My late-night solitude at the station rarely saw any disruption, save for the weekends.

My journey into teaching wasn't shaped by formal training in any way. Rather, it was an instinctive calling, prepped in tutorial sessions with classmates in high school and college. The notion of being a 'born teacher' resonated deeply within me, and I found a comfortable home. I keenly observed my teachers - their techniques, mannerisms, strategies, and responses. Little did I realize that this was a preparation for a career

I had not anticipated. My dreams, instead, were saturated with visions of becoming a priest, doctor, actor, or news reporter.

I understood the stress that a Teacher's sudden resignation just before the start of a new school year inflicts on a Principal. The task of finding a suitable replacement on short notice is a monumental challenge. Despite my own fear, the sheer elation at the opportunity compelled me to accept without a moment's hesitation.

"Would there be a problem in resigning?" he queried.

"Not as far as I know, Sir. But, I will check in the morning," I assured him.

The truth is I really didn't care if there were negative legal implications by resigning, despite only being there for five months. Teaching at SAC, the crown jewel of Bahamian high schools, held an allure that far surpassed the appeal of broadcast journalism.

The following morning I crafted a hand-written letter of resignation, the lines bleeding with a bittersweet blend of anticipation and farewell. I handed the draft to the receptionist requesting her to type it. Her refusal, born from disbelief or perhaps concern over losing a promising talent from ZNS, soon led to a summoning by Charles Carter, the Program Manager.

His cramped office, overflowing with files, records, tapes, and carts, reflected the clutter of emotions coursing through me. "They have great plans for you," he began, never clarifying who 'They' were, though I presumed it was the management, which naturally included him.

"TV is coming; you see the construction over there," pointing toward the vacant lot adjoining the ZNS studios. "You're one of the faces they're counting on. Besides, you're a natural. You can't go anywhere."

His words painted a picture of a developing broadcasting industry and my pivotal role in it. A huge mistake, he warned, emphasizing the gravity of my decision by referencing an interview I had conducted with the PLP's Cat Island Member of Parliament, Hon. Oscar Johnson. I was a novice reporter then, yet the penetrating questions I posed impressed him. The gathered media corps seemingly agreed, their silence allowing for an almost private interview.

Charles Carter was a media celebrity to young Bahamians like myself. His early morning weekday show was a staple during my high school years, and his popular Saturday "Young Bahamians Show" was a celebration of Bahamian identity through indigenous music and student features. Admiration and respect for him ran deep. He was a hero - young, intelligent, and host of the top radio morning show in the country.

Yet, the gravitational pull of the opportunity to teach at SAC was too strong. His ' attempted persuasion, despite compelling, could not deter me. The promise of television in an expanding broadcast industry was undoubtedly tempting, too But the vision of a PLP-governed ZNS was a discomforting prospect. I witnessed the occasional 'interference' in decisions regarding the selection of news stories, snatching those considerations from the journalistic integrity of the newsroom managers. Having the brief but extraordinarily beneficial insights into true journalism ethics at Xavier and Loyola, I sensed that my irritation with anything less than a professional journalism culture at ZNS would be intolerable.

I placated Charles with the assurance that I would 'think about it.' The words were hollow, a mere courtesy. There was no departure from my commitment to Mr. Adderley or the lure of a dream job. The thought of reneging never crossed my mind.

My mother's reaction to my impending career shift was one of sheer ecstasy. For her, as a former 'monitor' on her home island, my acceptance of a teaching position at the country's top high school was a shimmering feather in her metaphorical cap. Her fondness for the profession only amplified the joy of this new chapter in my life.

Life as an educator emerged as an exceptionally inflective juncture of my existence, only surpassed by one other experience. The revered Saint Augustine's College (SAC) had previously served as a fountain of knowledge for me. This incomparable learning journey had now come full circle: once in the phase of a blossoming student from 1964 to 1969, and again, ten years later, assuming the mantle of a teacher from 1974 to 1979. It was in these sacred halls that I imbibed the sacrosanct doctrine, virtues, and ethics of SAC, perhaps more intensely than any other person in its distinguished history. This powerful immersion molded me into an embodiment of SAC's spirit, a veritable SACer. Those valued years held up a mirror to my own self, shaping the core of my being in ways that continue to pulsate through my life.

Although I was without the conventional vestments of teacher training, I eagerly plunged into the unprofane arena of imparting knowledge. I sought to imitate, in my own pedagogical style, the style and methodologies of my former mentors who held an admired place in my heart: the Monks. Particularly, "The Bon", Father Leander Thompson, Father Alvin Fong Ben, and Deacon Lou Adderley.

In the intimate camaraderie of SAC, I and other respected colleagues like Sharon Storr, Arthur Fountain, and Preston Albury often reflected on the indelible impact the institution had on our lives. We marveled at its enduring effects on our minds and hearts. A shared sentiment gradually germinated within us, that it was at SAC where we first met men of superior intellectual depth, moral fibre, emotional capacity, physical prowess, and overarching competence. They were in stark contrast to any others we had known previously. Each Monk, for instance, held at least two Master's degrees, a rarity among the males of our family or community circles. Mr. Adderley added to the luster of these achievements by not only being one of the first native, black Bahamians to hold a college degree, but also by securing championships in tennis and wrestling at St. John's University. At SAC, his sporting prowess extended to baseball, basketball, and volleyball, later ascending to the role of coach of the Bahamas' national volleyball and basketball teams. Father Bonaventure, with his radiant intellect and eloquence, cast an awe-inspiring silhouette that left us young boys utterly mesmerized.

My tenure as a teacher offered me an enriched perspective of the English language, something that had eluded me though I was an outstanding English student. The revered mantle of a teacher weighed heavily upon me, instilling a deep-seated fear of any public action that might tarnish the integrity of this noblest of professions. I also realized the unique privilege that being a SAC student afforded, with its unparalleled emphasis on academia and sports, a legacy possibly only rivaled by the Government High School in the annals of Bahamian history.

Across a span of five rewarding years, I relished my role as a teacher and mentor. My dedication extended across the educational landscape of New Providence, beyond the SAC. The vibrant engagement with SAC students elevated my reputation among other schools. My coaching triumph with the 1975 Senior Girls Volleyball Team to a national championship, my refereeing of multiple sports, and my role as an emcee at inter-school events contributed to the narrative. Conversations among siblings, spread across different schools, further fueled my growing fame.

As the curtain of anonymity lifted, I found students and teachers from other schools equally fascinated by my persona. An emblematic encounter was with a young lady who sought me out after an inter-school softball game, where I served as an umpire. Extending her hand towards me, she shared her eagerness to meet 'in person' this "Mr. Lloyd everyone is talking about."

I harbored a fervent passion for SAC. I promoted it as the crown jewel among high schools in the country, and held its students in high regard, considering them among the most privileged, capable, and fortunate individuals in The Bahamas. I saw them as the well-chiseled products of a superior educational system. The Monks who founded SAC in the mid-1940s, true visionaries, appeared to me as prophetic geniuses. They journeyed from the upper mid-western United States to a country with whom they were largely unfamiliar. Immediately, they began a noble endeavor of establishing a school for underprivileged black boys.

During those times, quality educational opportunities for the average young native, regardless of race or gender, were scarce. The education they offered was beyond the wildest dreams of an average Bahamian youth. Father Silvan Bromenshenkel, the Monastery's second Prior, once recounted the backlash they faced from some in the established business communities, who scoffed at the Monks' belief in the intellectual potential of young, especially black Bahamian males, insisting that they were destined only for careers in manual labor. This prejudice induced a fierce defiance within the Monks, leading them to devise a curriculum that incorporated biology, chemistry, physics, mathematics, Latin, the classics, English, and more. They staunchly believed in the inevitable ascension of blacks, particularly males, to significant leadership roles within Bahamian society and the Catholic Church, and were determined to prepare them for such with a first-class education.

By the time I joined SAC as a student in the 60s, the institution had already earned an enviable reputation as the country's finest school. Moreover, by then, the wisdom of the Monks had already borne fruit, evident in the lives of alumni such as now deceased Fathers Bonaventure, Cletus, Boswell, Prosper, former Finance Minister, William Allen, Deacon Leviticus Adderley, and former professional baseball player and educator, Vincent Ferguson.

Two years into my teaching career at this venerable institution, another interesting chapter of my life unfolded: the blissful voyage of marriage.

SAC Teacher, 1977

Jeff teaching English Class

Directing SAC Students in a Drama
Production Rehearsal

Chapter Twelve

Marriage 1.0

Having a family was a long-desired objective of mine. I wanted children, but not in the fashion in which I and my siblings were conceived and raised – to single parents. For me, it was marriage or nothing else: no "shacking up", no children out-of-wedlock.

SAC's graduate, Shawn Bernadette Watkins, was a youthful force of nature, who exhibited an extraordinary level of maturity that belied her age. Her charismatic presence was impossible to ignore. Sometime after her graduation, our paths crossed leading to a romantic journey. On a frosty December morning, in 1977, our lives were bound together in matrimony.

The relationship inaugurated a vital period of personal growth and enlightenment for me. In the grand scheme of my life, it holds a profound significance, having forced me to confront my karmic debts while accelerating my journey toward maturity.

In retrospect, this first marriage was a catalyst, prompting a probing examination of my life's purpose. It made me aware that my true quest was to resolve this ancient, relationship-based debt. As the journey into the labyrinth of myself commenced, I soon appreciated that my ego was a masquerade that needed to be dismantled. For years, I allowed myself to be defined by the expectations of parents, elders, teachers, society, and others. My true identity was submerged under the smokescreen of these external standards, leaving me unfulfilled and unacquainted with my true self.

However, correspondent to the biblical prodigal son (Luke 15:17), this turbulent marital experience jolted me into a powerful self-realization. It unveiled my authentic identity, concealed beneath layers of pretense and superficiality. Despite the anguish and turmoil, a beautiful consequence emerged -- my firstborn child, Aisha Leta.

Within this experience, I rediscovered a long-forgotten habit – prayer. Late in 1978, I found myself fervently praying to the God of my youth, questioning His existence, and challenging Him to reveal Himself to me in a tangible way.

My prayer life, until that point, was irregular, at best. Church attendance was sporadic, a direct contrast to the routine visits of my childhood. Even while contemplating priesthood, I never truly cultivated a sincere prayer routine. However, those dark days evoked an earnest plea for divine intervention and a heartfelt cry for my Heavenly Father to rescue me from the whirlwind of life's disappointments.

Immediately following Aisha's 1978 birth, my desire to return permanently to the US, specifically New Orleans, intensified. Shawn aspired to pursue a college education, while I aimed for advanced degrees. As such, we started to explore options for emigration. The obstacle, however, was our perceived lack of qualifications. Successful emigration to the US required either established familial ties with a US citizen or resident, secure employment stateside, a special immigrant status, or a sponsor. Our situation didn't *seem* to meet any of these prerequisites, save for the potential sponsorship by my college friend, Cephas.

However, a conversation with Shawn's parents produced an unexpected lifeline. Her brother, Charlie, held US citizenship, an inheritance from his father, Robert Thornton, a US citizen himself. This sparked a glimmer of hope, the possibility of a pathway to our desired future. Armed with newfound optimism, we commenced the complex process of unraveling our potential migration. Robert, with his enthusiastic support and financial backing, proved to be an invaluable ally.

In January of 1979, with a heavy heart yet a hopeful spirit, I informed Mr. Adderley of my impending resignation. I expressed my intention to pursue higher education, setting a safety net for a potential return, if our plans fell through. Yet deep within, I was resolved to make the United States my permanent home. After six months of studious application processing, I boarded a plane in June 1979, leaving my homeland for the bustling city of New Orleans. Shawn and Aisha followed two months later.

Arriving in New Orleans, my heart pulsated with a blend of wild excitement, anticipation, and a dash of apprehension. We had finally embarked on the journey we had long dreamt of – one promising a menu of new experiences, opportunities, and challenges. Little did we know, that the road ahead would test our resolve in ways we could hardly anticipate.

I foresaw that our union required essential psychological, emotional, and psychic space to breathe, bloom, and fortify. It appeared improbable in The Bahamas. New Orleans was a familiar environment where I had a firm network of friends. This cultural epicenter felt as welcoming as an old glove, making it the obvious starting point for our journey in America. Furthermore, the shared aspiration of furthering our education and enlarging our horizons brought the promise of prosperity the US extended.

Shortly after our feet touched the streets of New Orleans, I became part of the South Central Bell (SCB) family – a subsidiary of the Bell Operating Systems. A couple of years down the line saw a promotion, setting the course for a thrilling career in telecommunications. The prestige and allure of a position at SCB was the desire of every employable individual in New Orleans. The lucrative remuneration and comprehensive benefits far exceeded those offered by most, if not all, businesses within Louisiana. It was the proverbial golden ticket to a rewarding lifetime career.

However, a jarring disturbance shook my professional journey in January 1982. A ruling from a Massachusetts court triggered the dismantling of the Bell System following a protracted legal battle with the US Justice

Department. This resulted in AT&T Corporation relinquishing control of the local telephone services provided by the Bell Operating Companies in the United States and Canada. Consequently, SCB transformed into an independent legal entity, prompting an immediate revision to my employment contract. The status of myself and hundreds of thousands of Bell System employees was thrown in doubt, leaving most without the benefits secured through the labour agreement with the Communications Workers of America (CWA).

I recall my supervisor summoning me to his office shortly after the news of the split to inform me of the new commission-based pay structure for sales staff. This seismic corporate shift led to a series of adjustments, including generous severance packages offered to veteran Bell employees, with many others reassigned within the SCB network. Parallel to the professional upheavals, the relocation appeared to have stoked the embers of our already strained marriage. The difficulties left us fatigued and dispirited.

The latter part of 1981 brought the devastating loss of both my parents within months of each other. My father succumbed to a heart attack in January, and my mother lost her battle with breast cancer in September. Despite my earnest wish for it to endure, the marriage seemed destined for failure. It just wasn't to be. The finalization of our divorce felt like a sharp knife of failure that tormented me for years following. Even though my parents had separated early in my life, and other family members, too, had chosen different paths, I yearned to break this cycle.

My siblings and I grew up as children of separated parents which proved desperately challenging. We often found ourselves unwitting pawns in the power struggles, stuck in the throes of conflicts that pitted one parent against the other. The bitter resentment my father harbored towards my mother bore heavily on me. His attempts to restrict my interactions with her were particularly harsh. My desire to visit her was mostly met with denial, save for the occasional grudging concession when confronted by my grandmother or a visiting relative about his perceived unfairness. A memory of Uncle Alfred, my father's brother, comes to mind.

"Stanford, why are you preventing this boy from seeing his Ma??" he exclaimed on one such occasion, the irritation palpable in his voice as he observed my heartache upon being denied permission to visit her. Uncle Alfred was a stern, slim man, with a grave demeanor that rarely indulged in laughter or trivial banter. His words carried the gravitas of command, and even my stoic father found it prudent not to challenge his younger brother's authority. His influence on our household was clearly evident that Sunday afternoon.

The bitter rivalries and parental separations ignited in me a drive to create a much different and better life for myself. The notion of becoming an unwed parent, or maintaining a superficial relationship, seemed to me an insulting profound disservice to the sacred bond of matrimony. I could not articulate these feelings then, but they stirred within me, nonetheless. My parents' separation left me with a lingering sense of hurt, shame, disappointment, and confusion. The emotional turmoil spurred my resolve to ensure that I, and any future offspring, would never endure such pain.

This deep-rooted motivation to rise above my lineage's traditions propelled me to envision a future where my children would bask in the warmth of a loving and empowering home atmosphere, led by committed, affectionate, supportive parents, dedicated to the sacred vocations of marriage and parenthood. However, as destiny would have it, I suffered the very thing I dreaded most – divorce. The thought of my daughter undergoing the harsh repercussions of our failed marriage haunted me desperately.

In November 1982, I found myself in the serene ambiance of a bare New Orleans courtroom, surrendered to the guidance of my young lawyer. The judge's confirmatory questions were met with my affirmative responses, and within a span of ten minutes, a bond that was meant to be a union of love, joy, commitment, and shared sorrows was legally dissolved. The aftermath left me with a bewildering amalgam of emotions – sadness, relief, shame, and uncertainty.

However, a popular adage from my youth echoed in my mind, "When one door closes, another opens." True to these words, life opened a new chapter, one that held the promise of powerful transcendence.

Communications Consultant, South Central Bell, La.
1980.

Chapter Thirteen

Divine Awakening

In the cradle of my youth, I was nurtured by the stringent beliefs of fundamentalist religion. The edicts of this faith were underpinned by unforgiving authoritarianism, cloaked in a spirit of legalism and peppered with fear, jealousy, judgment and eternal damnation. The doctrine was unbending, coupled with a rigid interpretation of the Judeo-Christian scripture that was applied with uncompromising literalism. This God was portrayed as jealous, vindictive, and selective with 'chosen' and 'unchosen' people. Those He deemed unchosen, he obliterated. Those chosen, he protected. This faith claimed the mantle of 'truth', advocating an undistracted pathway of life, which was to be staunchly defended against the encroachments of other religions, traditions, or secularism. It was a realm of stark polarity. A dogged assertion held sway – "You are either with us or against us".

Within this stranglehold of belief system, I found myself burdened with an oppressive sense of guilt, ignominy, unworthiness, and an overwhelming consciousness of sinfulness. I was overwhelmed by a debilitating sense of helplessness, at the mercy of God's compassion for salvation. The fear of divine punishment served as a coercive tether that kept me adhering to the faith, to escape the incineration of hell and eternal damnation. The only thread of hope was belief in Jesus Christ, offering the sole possibility of salvation. I was indoctrinated to hold the Bible, a singular holy book, as the infallible, inerrant word of God, which demanded literal obedience. To my juvenile mind, bowing to the stern injunctions of this religion seemed the only path to survival. The alternative was a hellish existence, unending suffering under the devil's cruel torment.

However, as I aged, a conundrum emerged. The Bible I was taught to believe in, whose God seemed prejudiced against certain people, was also the Bible that proclaimed God as "Father of all, who is over all and through all and in all" (Ephesians 4:6 NAB). It also stated that "there is no partiality with God." (Romans 2:11). It went on to record Jesus as saying that "He came that we could have life and have it to the full". (John 10:10). These and many other similar passages revealed an inconsistency that I found difficult to reconcile, especially the 'chosen' and 'unchosen' parts.

As I matured, I found this religious façade incompatible with my amplified consciousness. The God of this faith seemed more and more incoherent with each passing day. The narrative that painted an all-good, all-knowing, all-powerful, and all-just God who, at the same time, was also jealous and selective was baffling. 'He' seemed too imbued with human traits and weaknesses to be a divine entity.

Yet, amidst this intellectual turmoil, a peculiar desire surfaced within me. I still felt an inexplicable urge to become a Catholic priest. Despite my profound misgivings and discomfort with the teachings presented to me as biblical or religious truths, a 'calling' to be an ordained minister of the Gospel of Jesus Christ continued to circulate within me.

However, I was ensnared in the chains of my beliefs. The terror of eternal damnation still exerted its iron grip on me. The construct of my thoughts refused to entertain any alternative viewpoint, even though my frustrations and anxieties were simmering, ready to erupt.

Even the potency of Holy Scriptures began to diminish in my life, as I dove into various Bible classes in college. The multiple contradictions I unearthed – from the dual stories of creation, the two Genesis accounts of Noah, to the contrasting narratives of the resurrection – led me to question the 'inerrancy' of the word of God.

Transformation

My spiritual evolution, however, took an abrupt and unexpected turn. Without consciously aware of it, over the years, the spiritual soil of my life had been meticulously tilled – whether at the fervent 'street meetings' of my youth, the impassioned revivals at the Fowler Street Church of God in Nassau, the many reflective retreats and contemplative days of silence I attended in high school and college, or the numerous in-depth discussions I had with priests and ministers whilst discerning my calling. These experiences served to intensify my spiritual thirst.

Beginning with my enrolment in high school, some in my family believed that I harbored aspirations for the priesthood. This conjecture only gained momentum when I left for college. It was there, amidst the sobriety of theological study, that my intrigue and commitment towards priesthood deepened. Despite marriage in 1977, the allure of the ordained ministry lingered.

As I have previously divulged, the strain of the marital tension eventually led me to implore God to reveal Himself to me if He was indeed the ultimate truth. This fervent plea reached its crescendo in a life-altering event in November 1982, in the quiet solitude of my home on Law Street, New Orleans.

Before that life-altering event, I barely knew of Eastern spiritual practices such as meditation, yoga, chanting, and the like. The term 'divine awakening' was alien to me. I was taught to think of God as a being in the sky, beyond the reach of my outstretched contact. Though, I heard of the "made in the image and likeness of God', that term was a distant concept unable to penetrate my puerile understanding. I never fully understood that having the 'likeness of God" meant that his nature co-existed with mine; that I was of the same essence as God; that, like the Hindus who believe the inner man (Atman) is of the same essence with God (Brahman), the Christian practices of prayer, fasting, worship, and almsgiving were spiritual disciplines that were meant to help me identify what is false and uncover what is real – God Himself/Itself.

However, that all began to change one afternoon when I was introduced to a college professor, Peter Leduff, at a mutual friend's house. He exuded a compelling serenity and seemed to 'have it all together', personifying the eminent qualities I had longed to have. He reminded me of the influential Msgr. Preston Moss, my spiritual director, who significantly impacted my life. Shortly after our meeting, in October 1982, he invited me to an evening yoga session at a residence in Metairie, Louisiana. The weekly gathering entailed chanting, discourse by a Yoga Master, and a short meditation. The experience, however, was not what I had expected. When envisioning 'yoga', I imagined individuals in extravagant, oversized, colorful attire, contorting themselves into pretzel-like postures. Contrary to my preconceived notions, the session was nothing like that.

Instead, I witnessed an elderly Indian gentleman, whose strange Hindi lecture was being translated by a young Indian girl. While his discourse largely eluded my understanding, the meditation instructions he provided, also printed on a card I received that evening, left a distinct impression on my mind.

By this time, I had resigned from my position at SCB to begin an entrepreneurial project with my friend, Barry Bonner. We operated a cards enterprise, named Greetings Cards, Inc., that represented several prominent greeting card companies, including the well-known Gibson Cards of Cincinnati, Ohio, whose product line included a series named

Pleasant Thoughts that featured the popular writings of the late Helen Steiner Rice.

In the course of our business, I traversed every corner of Louisiana, marketing our cards. In our initial eight months, we generated a respectable $36,000, enabling us to purchase a truck, and supplies, and provide temporary employment for a few high school students. One such student, Wallace Lord, and his family, became an extension of my own.

By our agreement, I worked full-time in the business, while Barry assisted with accounting and other tasks as they arose. Also by agreement in compensation for my full-time commitment, he generously allowed me free rent on the other side of his 1948 Law Street house. Our second year, 1983, saw a significant financial leap, grossing over $170,000, primarily due to the overwhelming sales of seasonal cards and the popular Helen Steiner Rice product line.

Though 'disappointed' with the evening of yoga to which Peter had invited me, I was, nevertheless, quite impressed with the idea of meditation. Thus, several weeks after that session, while entertaining Aisha on her fortnightly visit with me, I decided to 'try' this meditation, as instructed.

Accordingly, once Aisha was comfortably nestled in bed after an evening of some revelry with Barry's children, I positioned myself in the posture prescribed by the yoga Teacher, placed my palms on my thighs, closed my eyes, and gently turned my attention to my breathing. Almost in an instant, I was transported at an exceedingly high rate of speed through an eerily dark tunnel enveloped by what appeared to be dynamically pulsating waves of energy on each side. As I traveled, a shimmering blue speck, like a luminous light, far in the distance, appeared before me, becoming larger as I moved closer. As I approached, and came to a stop, I noticed that the blue image was, in fact, a lake of indescribable beauty and essence, scintillating with billowing wave-like movements. Interestingly, even shockingly, on the other side of the lake stood two beings whom I recognized immediately – my parents, both who had died a year earlier. My mother stood on my right, and my father on my left. Mom, garbed in a blue outfit, began motioning toward me with firm gesticulations, saying: "Son, you will be a great man one day, but you have to change your way of living". Her communication was not actual words, but, rather, an energetic transmission of information. Besides the staccato hand movement, she and my father were virtually impassive. Her 'words' that blessed night were the exact ones the street preacher had told me decades earlier.

As uncannily as I had been transported to the 'lake', with the completion of my mother's instructions', I began a retreat with the same frenetic acceleration as I traveled before, while the lake before me grew smaller and smaller, while the outlines of my parents became less and less distinct. Upon awakening from this experience, my heart pounded as if it was going to burst my chest. The entire affair seemed to last only a few minutes, but I was shocked to discover that it had taken over two hours.

Frightened beyond comprehension, and though it was now well past midnight, I immediately phoned Peter to relay the news, my hands trembling with fear, excitement, and a self-consciousness I had never known before. He was ecstatic, praising me for the 'breakthrough' I had just encountered. I told him that I felt as if I had 'died'. I spoke more truthfully than I understood, for, indeed, I did 'die' that blessed November night. A new "Me" emerged from that encounter. I then understood, and had, indeed, experienced, the 'divine' awakening' that Peter later described. The experience was so profound, so mysterious, and powerfully transformative that words fail to capture the depth and breadth of what happened that evening.

Overnight, my perception of reality fundamentally shifted. When I arose the following morning, it was as if I was walking on air, my feet not touching the ground. I sensed an existence beyond the physical boundaries of my body; that I was one with all that is, and ever was. My desire for food virtually disappeared. Concomitantly, my dietary preferences changed in an instant, no longer with an appetite for flesh, dairy, or processed foods. I embarked on extended fasting periods, driven not by a conscious decision but by the true absence of hunger. It felt as though I was nourished solely by the air I breathed. I developed an intense interest in all things **spiritual** literature, music, and talks and voraciously ingested as much of them as I could find, including titles such as Cosmic Consciousness and The Autobiography of a Yogi. Additionally, I regularly attended the weekly yoga sessions Peter introduced me to weeks earlier, and Sunday services at the Unity Church in New Orleans. Over time, one book gripped my attention with a riveting attachment: Thomas Merton's *"New Seeds of Contemplation"*. It served, in essence, as my spiritual bible. Within its pages, I found passages that deeply resonated with me, such as:

"If I never become what I was meant to be, but always remain what I am not, I shall spend eternity contradicting myself by being at once something and nothing, a life that wants to live and is dead, a death that wants to be dead and cannot quite achieve its own death because it still has to exist."

Another read: "From the moment that we have responded by faith and charity to His Love for us, a supernatural union of souls with His Indwelling Divine Person gives us a participation in his Divine sonship and nature. A 'new being' is brought into existence. I become a 'new man' and this new man, spiritually and mystically one identity, is at once Christ and myself."

Moreover, one passage required substantial contemplation for me to fully assimilate: "Therefore, when you and I become what we are really meant to be, we will discover not only that we love one another perfectly but that we are both living in Christ and Christ in us, and we are all one Christ."[1]

The Bible, too, proved an inexhaustible wellspring. A newfound understanding of its metaphysical subtleties leaped from its pages. I was suffused with a sense of impenetrable tranquility, security, and divine benevolence. It was as though I inhabited a celestial realm enfolded by a benevolent presence and a deeply woven feeling of connection to all creation and an all-encompassing, transcendent love.

In the subsequent months, I caught glimpses of the spiritual potential dormant within me. The revelations were nothing short of awe-inspiring. If there was ever a moment when I was 'ready' for spiritual awakening, it was that auspicious November moment. I had longed for a deeper understanding of the unifying power of love, peace, and harmony within the world and myself. As a consequence of this life-altering experience, I felt an intensified urge to devote my life to the betterment of humanity and the blossoming of the divine essence inherent in all beings. This spiritual epiphany was the gateway to me realizing my highest potential and embodying the divine entity inherently residing within me.

As time passed, following this monumental spiritual initiation, I began entertaining thoughts of returning home, fueled greatly by frequent conversations with siblings about the declining state of our family affairs since our mother's passing. I felt a moral obligation to intervene and restore harmony. Hence, in the summer of 1983, I targeted the summer of 1984 as my intended date of return.

---

1. MERTON, Thomas New Seeds of Contemplation, 1961, The Abbey of Gethsemani

CHAPTER FOURTEEN

Homeward Bound

1984 MARKED A PIVOTAL period of change and growth for me. The end of a marriage and mind-bending mystical experience paved the way for a fresh start. It led me from the lively city of New Orleans to the sandy beaches of The Bahamas, where I was tasked with refashioning my life and establishing a source of income. As the summer of my homecoming approached, I exercised a detailed plan to avoid hasty choices while keeping in sight the weight of my decisions. An especially significant consideration was the impact of my departure on six-year-old Aisha. Despite the fracture in my marriage, my commitment to fatherhood remained steadfast. I felt an urgent obligation to retain a warm, close relationship with her.

Naturally, teaching was the most feasible career option, given my expertise and the ever-present demand for educators. My preference veered towards private institutions, so I promptly initiated the application process for the upcoming school year. A dear friend and mentor, Vincent Ferguson, became my touchstone in this new endeavor. He was the Principal of Aquinas College, and while he held no power in the hiring decision, he directed me to Sister Maedeen Russell, OSB, at the Catholic School Board of Education.

Vince was an inspirational figure to me, someone I long admired for his qualities as a person and leader. As a high school student, I was intrigued by his professional baseball career in the United States, despite having never met him. We later worked together when he served as the President of the Bahamas Amateur Basketball Association (BABA) and I as the Secretary-General. In September 1984, through his support and endorsement, I joined Aquinas College's faculty, rekindling the professional relationship that we established six years earlier. However, the initial joy was short-lived. Consequently, I began exploring alternate career options.

Immediately upon my return to the Bahamas, I sought out and found a similar gathering of the weekly yoga sessions that I attended in New Orleans. The host family, Tony Wallas and his wife, Cathie, soon became close friends. While searching for a possible career change, Tony extended a helping hand in this endeavor by inviting me to apply for a vacancy at the General Agency (GA) that he managed. The New York-based Colgate Palmolive Company, for whom GA was the local Agency, sought a country manager to rejuvenate their declining sales portfolio. Tony believed I was perfect for the role despite my late application. My past experience with SCB was my saving grace, as it made me familiar with the workings of an American Fortune 500 company, a trait that Colgate's management appreciated.

At SCB, I had been thoroughly trained in sales performance and management. Although my knowledge of personal care products was limited, the universal principles of sales and marketing were applicable across industries. Immediately, I recognized the need for effective market stimulation, especially for products that had underperformed in the Bahamian market for as long as Colgate did.

Colgate was up against stiff competition from Crest and Proctor & Gamble, but with the right strategy, I knew we could reclaim a sizeable market share. The name Colgate already had a profound presence in the Bahamian psyche such that any toothpaste, regardless of brand, was referred to as 'Colgate'. When I joined GA in November 1986, the annual sales were a meager four hundred and fifty thousand dollars ($450,000). But by the time I departed nine years later, we had achieved a staggering three hundred percent increase, with consistent annual sales exceeding one million, two hundred thousand dollars ($1,200,00)

During my tenure, GA was acquired by Thompson Trading (TT), a food and beverage distributor with a broader market reach. Although initially apprehensive, I was reassured by Colgate that my position as their country manager would remain unchanged. This arrangement was beneficial for both GA and TT, as they received leadership support from me beyond my responsibilities with Colgate, especially in human resource matters, all the while Colgate shouldered my remuneration and benefits.

Despite the success and security of my employment, a gnawing entrepreneurial desire began to intensify within me. I wanted more than just a salaried position, and was eager to explore my potential beyond the confines of my employment then. The path toward this self-employment pursuit was nurtured by my Rotary colleague, Dr. Jonathan "Johnny" Rodgers, a successful entrepreneur himself. He was moved by my assertive stance during discussions in Rotary, respecting the diligence and ethics I applied to all my Rotarian responsibilities. At one of our regular Tuesday lunches, he introduced the concept of a joint business venture. My heart fluttered with a powerful rush of exhilaration at the proposition.

Thus, in 1994, in partnership with Johnny and Dionisio D'Aguilar, whom I'd met through my work with Colgate, we embarked on an entrepreneurial journey with the Canadian franchise, Pizza Pizza. After a four-month training at Pizza Pizza's headquarters in Toronto, we opened two branches in New Providence. However, the venture, while full of promise, turned out to be more of a challenging learning curve than a profitable enterprise. The business struggled to compete with the dominant franchises like Domino's, even though we firmly believed that our pizza was superior. Ironically, we gained recognition not for our pizza, but for our chicken. While this distinction differentiated us from our competitors, our main product, pizza, failed to make its mark. As a consequence, the business teetered on the brink of failure, causing a strain in my friendship with Johnny.

However, despite its failure, the experience provided me with invaluable insights and knowledge. Never having had much business experience, I stumbled to find secure entrepreneurial footing. Though it may have appeared as a misfortune, I actually learned a lot about running a business, especially managing people, forecasting sales, understanding the tastes and proclivities of customers, and, most especially, learning how to navigate the sometimes anxiety-produced expectations of one's superiors or business partners.

Eventually, my friendship with Johnny was restored, rebounding to not just recover, but also grow stronger and deeper. We survived the ordeal with a deeper understanding and respect for each other, ultimately strengthening our bond. It's in adversity, after all, that we truly come to know ourselves and those around us.

Chapter Fifteen

Marriage 2.0

THE CADENCE OF MY spiritual journey escalated as I crossed the threshold of my ancestral nation. Under the patient guidance of Fr. Elias Achatz, OSB, I dedicated myself without reservation to once again explore the potential of a priesthood vocation. I found solace and purpose in the cloistered confines of the monastery, immersing in its tranquility on many weekends, the litmus test of my newly-revived inclination.

Simultaneously, a powerful yearning for the contentment of familial life warmed the chambers of my heart. Yet, it was critical first to authenticate the legitimacy of my priestly pull, warding off the intervention of any other aspiration during this 'final' examination of possible ecclesiastical commitment. My heart danced with a vivid aspiration, a purpose to return home as a radar of significant influence, a torchbearer of hope for my people.

In July 1986, an invitation from Fr. Elias led me to the serene embrace of The Jesuit Spirituality Center in Grand Coteau, Louisiana, which was renowned for its 3, 5, 8, or 30-day retreats, based on the Spiritual Exercises of St. Ignatius Loyola. The eerie silence and solitude of the place served as the perfect arena for focused introspection. I spent an entire month, a long enough stretch of uninterrupted quiet to discern God's whisper regarding my existential crossroads: Marriage, Priesthood, or Dedicated Single?

Just a year before, Bernadette Louise Cooper, someone I long knew, stepped into my life, adding vibrant hues to my discernment process. Concurrently, Monsignor Moss undertook an investigation of the canonical procedures towards a potential ordination, should I choose to tread that path. My story was knotted with complexities: a divorcee, and the father of a six-year-old. During a conference in Rome that summer, he explored possibilities, only to discover that I had to wait until Aisha reached her twenty-third birthday before the church *could consider* my case. Though it may have appeared as a disappointment, and I certainly considered it so at the time, I perceived God's message as a 'not now' rather than an outright 'no'.

Even though the priesthood lost its magnetism, the commitment to deepen my spiritual journey was beyond challenge, without an iota of doubt or reservation. It was a sacred pact with myself. However, as time progressed and amidst the spiritual ebb and flow, family life slowly emerged as my true life's calling, although the ordained ministry continued to hold a mysterious allure. Meeting Bernadette, ignited an incremental desire to be married again.

Our connection was like the seamless confluence of two rivers, natural and effortless. We were bound by the threads of childhood friendship, and a deep connection between our families, not only as neighbors but through blossoming romantic ties. My brother Charlie and Bern's sister, Charlene, were past sweethearts, and Agatha, her other sister, once held my romantic interest. A second marital voyage with Bern, I expected, would be a stark contrast to my first. For starters, I was anchored in my spiritual pursuits and was far more self-aware.

Bern, much like myself, was a product of the ghetto. We spoke the same 'language', navigating our way through life's idiosyncrasies with which we were both familiar. Upon our re-aquaintance, I was already a father, and she was a mother, with a daughter, the lovely Kendra Abigail. Following a courtship of three harmonious years, we exchanged our vows on February 20, 1988, at St. Bede's Catholic Church, her home parish. Almost immediately, we eagerly embarked on the journey of parenthood. By then, the sands of time had accumulated to mark six years since my divorce, and as a man in my mid-30s, I was keen not to delay the continuing joys and responsibilities of fatherhood. Bern, who had gracefully transitioned into her third decade of life, also shared this longing to add to our family. For me, her daughter was mine, as my daughter was hers. There was no demarcation into step-child this or that. For, as the biblical mandate prescribed that the two shall become one, which I earnestly believed, it meant for me the acceptance and embrace of all that she was and to which she was biologically and psychically connected. A mere eighteen months post our nuptials, we nested in our own abode, conveniently located just a stone's throw away from my mother's dwelling. My heart had always been tethered to central New Providence.

Securing my own home marked a substantial milestone in my life's journey, reflecting my growth, maturity, and accomplishments. This objective has piqued my interest since the spring of my youth. The wisdom of our elders, like the steady rhythm of a drum, had ingrained in us the cultural imperative of property ownership. Their voices rang in our ears from the first job and paycheck, urging us to 'invest in a piece of land.' Homeownership was a vital strand in our cultural fabric. It held a lofty position, right next to education - the two sacred obligations of my generation. "Earn your education. Own your house." - the mantras of our lives.

My union with Bernadette unfolded like the changing tides, a quantum difference from my previous marriage. It prompted my sister, Christina, to reflect that this should have been the 'first and only one.' Her words unveiled more than she perhaps intended, voicing the silent consensus of my family since the dawn of my first marriage. My matrimonial bond with Bernadette radically shifted the course of my life. However, little did I know what a shift it would be; for looming on the horizon was a series of dramatic events that would consume the rest of our wedded life.

Strange Illness

Our tale took an unseen turn with the conception of our second child - our darling, Shakti. We long desired a pair of siblings, ideally close in age. Shakti's arrival, however, presented an array of challenges from the outset, pushing her mother into the confines of bed for the majority of the pregnancy.

Morning sickness is no stranger to many women during their first trimester of pregnancy, presenting itself through waves of nausea or bouts of vomiting, often undeterred by the hour of the day. In Bern's case, this discomfort spanned the entire pregnancy, persisting right up until Shakti's birth in the United States in June 1990. We chose the United States as the place of birth, primarily because we intended to relocate there at some future date.

In a twist of events, Shakti couldn't wait for the safe confines of a hospital room. She instead made her grand entrance on the busy highway in Hollywood, Florida, as the ambulance pulled over to assist in her impatient delivery. This unusual birth spectacle attracted a slew of news crews from various media outlets, all eager to catch a word with Bern, who, understandably, was utterly exhausted from the grueling labor and delivery ordeal.

However, mere months after Shakti's birth, Bern's health began to deteriorate, couched in a mystery that left local medical experts perplexed. She was a woman who always radiated vitality, yet now appeared increasingly gaunt. Despite her naturally slim figure, especially for her statuesque 5'8" height, she could ill-afford any further weight loss. No physical impairment had prefigured her dramatic unfolding, yet something was unmistakably awry. Still, she bore her suffering with a fortitude that only surfaced in complaints when the pain was almost unbearable.

Throughout our courtship, she was an epitome of health, remarkably untouched by commonplace ailments like the flu, the common cold, or diarrhea. So, witnessing her health take a turn for the worse, despite having successfully birthed three children, was confounding.

Concurrently, our marriage was evolving into a unified spiritual entity. This being her first foray into the marital journey, she seemed to draw unconsciously from her parents' wedded blueprint, holding their fidelity and commitment as the paragon of marital responsibility. Their well-established marital and parental roles, prescribed by societal norms, had her mother, Harriet Smith-Cooper, at the helm of the household, while her father was the family's breadwinner. Harriet's commanding presence and dominating spirit were a source of stern authority, remaining unchallenged and unquestioned.

By mid-June of 1991, it was obvious that Bern needed urgent medical attention. Initially, the symptoms presented as difficulty swallowing, gradually devolving into chronic diarrhea. Her weight loss was now alarmingly rapid and drastic.

A local, renowned gastroenterologist conducted examinations but found no evident anomalies. Despite this, it was clear something was seriously amiss. Her significant weight loss over a brief period was a screaming testament to this fact. In a desperate attempt for answers, she was referred to a Florida-based gastroenterologist at Mt. Sinai Medical Center. Weighing a mere fifty-eight pounds when she arrived that August 1991 afternoon, she was at the door of death. Swiftly, a team of seasoned specialists assembled, managing to halt her perilous slide toward impending doom. After several days of rigorous examinations, the culprit was identified as collagenous colitis, a rare disease affecting fewer than one hundred individuals worldwide at that time. This revelation was novel to our local Bahamian doctors. The medical literature, scarce in its available coverage, defined it as an inflammation of the colon, a subtype of colitis, which induced chronic diarrhea, primarily in middle-aged women. Mt Sinai's specialists opined that the condition's nature rendered it invisible in routine colonoscopies, only revealing itself under the microscopic scrutiny of a biopsy. The exact cause remained elusive, but it seemed to be a cocktail of genetic and environmental factors.

The hardships imposed by unending medical treatments, persisting financial woes, and the daunting task of tending to an ailing spouse, whose condition steadily worsened, seemed insurmountable. Additionally, I had the care of two young children, Shiva, at a tender thirty months, and Shakti, barely a year old.

Despite these hardships, our marital journey remained remarkably harmonious. Regardless of the relentless health battles and the consequential challenges they presented, there prevailed a profound, unspoken understanding that this marriage was preordained.

Regrettably, due to the incessant diarrhea induced by her colitis, her kidneys ultimately failed, necessitating yet another medical program, dialysis. Each episode of her health rollercoaster oscillated between stretches of manageable tranquility to critically threatening periods of varying lengths. During one of these periods, she surprised us with the news of her pregnancy. Despite my initial shock, I assured her of my joy and pride. This was startling, not just due to the prospect of becoming a parent in my late 40s, but that doctors previously confirmed that her reproductive years had long been claimed by her illness, making pregnancy seem impossible. Yet with her health hanging by a thread, she now carried another life within her.

Newborn

At approximately 4 p.m. on a late autumn Thursday, November 29th, I was led to the neo-natal unit of the historic Princess Margaret Hospital, to meet our premature newborn. I found myself standing before an incubator, looking at the tiny being protected within, so small and dark that I initially thought the nurses had made an error.

"No, Nurse," I remember asserting with polite confusion, "I'm here for Jeffrey Lloyd's baby."

"That's your baby, Mr. Lloyd", Nurse Knowles calmly retorted, her tone solemn with certainty as she pointed towards the incubator mere inches away.

"Get ready, hold her. You need to hold her," Nurse Knowles added, opening the incubator's side as I readied myself to receive our miniature human child.

The infant was as black as the midnight sky. Seeing her for the first time, my mind struggled to comprehend the miracle of life, evident in such a small being. She seemed impossibly delicate, impossibly alive. Nurses moved around us in a well-rehearsed dance, one of them unpacking a set of hospital garments. "Let's get this on you," one said, her words preparing me for what was to come.

The weight of the situation held me captive. I stood there, draped in hospital garb, my body trembling with anticipation and apprehension. As our tiny daughter was gently placed into my arms, I found myself in awe. Her slender fingers were like thin spaghetti, her tiny form fitting neatly into my right palm with room to spare. She weighed a mere 1.1 lbs. The nurses stood by, seemingly prepared for my imminent collapse.

There she was, Sanjay Maria, asleep and utterly still in my arms, her silence expanding the moment into an eternity. I prayed silently for her survival, having never before witnessed life in such a small and vulnerable form.

Having been ordained a Permanent Deacon on June 21st, just five months prior, I returned the next morning and baptized her. Despite her tiny frame, her hunger prompted energetic, aggressive wriggles from her miniature form. For 12 long weeks, she remained in the incubator, eventually emerging as a healthy, 5-pound baby. Once home, I dedicated myself wholly to her care, permitting no one else to administer the intensive attention she needed in those critical months. Today, as a young adult, she exhibits no visible signs of her early dance with destiny.

Forging A New Path

In the ensuing five years after Sanjay's birth, Bern's life plunged into a vortex of hospital stays and surgeries, serving as a scary reminder of the early '90s. With her health steadily deteriorating, the uninterrupted emotional, physical, and financial toll made life almost unbearable.

On a fateful Thursday morning, August 30th, 2007, she returned home from dialysis complaining of an excruciating headache. Despite our best efforts and medical support, her condition worsened, culminating in a massive stroke. She died two days later.

The latter years of her life were a bittersweet symphony of pain and struggle interwoven with immense joy, humor, dedication, and an untiring faith in God. After years of battling her disease, she was finally at peace. Her life was a testament to her faith, courage, and resilience leaving a permanent mark on our family, friends, and community.

Naturally, our children's lives were greatly affected by their mother's sickness. In September 2007, at the age of 55, I found myself a widower and the sole caretaker of three minor daughters, the youngest of whom, Sanjay, was barely six years old. Shiva joined me at the YEAST Institute, postponing her college plans by a year. Shakti was still in high school, and Sanjay only beginning second grade.

By this point, with thirty years of adulthood behind me, I had weathered two challenging marriages, each teaching me valuable lessons about myself and life. Despite the apparent misfortunes, I still held firmly the belief that married life was a blessing. However, in the immediacy of Bern's death, the commitment to my children was paramount. Now thrust into the sole responsibility of raising my daughters, I felt a sense of purposeful resolve. Nothing would interfere with my obligations as a father. Raising my children became my singular mission, my primary duty, and my personal assignment.

Chapter Sixteen

Fatherhood

The adage goes, "Parenting is a reflection of how you were parented," subtly implying the inevitable replica of inherited lessons in one's approach to raising their children. This cycle of life held true for me, as my blueprints for parenting were extracted from the examples primarily of Grandma and Dad, but many others whose lives I keenly observed. Their principles of parenting, as if seared into my subconscious, steered my decisions as a father, even today.

Their formula was founded on the pillars of discipline, diligence, industry, self-governance, manners, and most importantly, a belief in the timeless wisdom expressed in the Book of Ecclesiastes, that there was a time for everything under the sun. They championed the notion that all individuals, regardless of their societal standing, deserved respect.

As a father, an intuitive understanding blossomed within me, that I was the towering presence in my children's universe, a potent influence shaping their world. I was my daughters' first love story, their inaugural mentor. The manner in which I executed this monumental responsibility, I reasoned, would form the foundation of their self-perception and comprehension of the world.

Reflecting on my formative years, the common representation of fatherhood was a contaminated one, far from the ideals I wanted to enflesh. Mainstream media, television shows, and movies were bereft of authentic paternal figures, absent the fidelity and commitment that I envisioned as intrinsic to a father's role. Instead, the media paraded a spectacle of volatile relationships, replete with undisciplined passions and blatant disregard for even the most basic societal norms. This profile, in my view, muddled the understanding of masculine and feminine identity for the younger generation. The unfortunate prevalence of domestic violence painted masculinity as perilous and toxic, a trait to be dodged, offering no benefits to the family dynamic. This corrosive image, portrayed as abusive, unreliable, and domineering, seemed to impair men's ability to form genuine relationships with women and children.

In an era where masculinity was equated with harmful behavior, it posed a challenge to raising wholesome children. Oddly enough, some women condoned such behavior, resulting in a cycle of pain and destruction. The notion of manhood entwined with fatherhood, whether physical or spiritual, demanded a synergy with women who comprehended the needs of the human soul.

Femininity and masculinity, I believe, are more than mere gender roles; they represent a way of being. Some execute these roles better than others, obviously. However, when a man's approach to fatherhood doesn't align with God's ideal, it naturally deprives his children of the unique energy and perspective that his presence can provide. I pledged to myself, early on, that I would stand among those who would uplift fatherhood to the pedestal of respect and dignity it deserved. This solemn vow became my guiding star, directing my journey as a father.

Fatherhood, in my view, wasn't merely an obligation, but a sacred responsibility that illuminates the path to maturity. It's a role that brings with it challenges that force one to rise above oneself, fostering adaptability, and teaching invaluable lessons about love, life, and sacrifice. It has become for me an invitation to share in the gift of creation and the joy of nurturing a soul from innocence to wisdom.

As I strove to fulfill my pledge, I reflected on my upbringing, reviewing the virtues Grandma and Dad had instilled in me. Discipline was not just about enforcing rules, but about cultivating proficient self-management. Hard work was not simply about achieving success, but about understanding the value of perseverance and the satisfaction of a job well done. Respect for all was not merely about good manners, but recognizing the inherent dignity and worth of every individual.

I considered that being a father was more than providing guidance and setting an example, but, rather, being present in a child's life, bearing witness to their triumphs and failures, their joys and sorrows; about offering unconditional love and support, even when they make mistakes;

and demonstrating, through actions more than words, what it means to be a man of integrity, kindness, and compassion.

In the distorted narrative of masculinity perpetuated by media and societal misconceptions, I felt an urgent need for men to reclaim the noble aspects of masculinity. To rise against the tide of negative masculinity and demonstrate that strength is not about domination, but about protection, that leadership is not about control, but about service, and that true manhood is not about avoiding responsibilities, but about embracing them wholeheartedly.

I strove to leave a peerless example of this noble cause, promoting a healthier vision of fatherhood, and through it, a more balanced understanding of masculinity. I've endeavored to provide a living testament to the powerful impact a responsible, loving father can have in his children's lives, and on the world around him.

When I look back on my journey, I wish not just to be remembered as a father who did his best, but as a man who upheld the sanctity of fatherhood, recognizing and cherishing it as the esteemed and dignified role it deserves to be. Through my journey, I aim to inspire others to embrace fatherhood not as a burden, but as a gift, a privilege, and most importantly, an opportunity to leave a lasting legacy of love, wisdom, fidelity, and strength for generations to come.

Chapter Seventeen

Marriage – Vehicle of Self Discovery

By September 2007, two chapters of my life closed with the passing of Bern and the effective end of my second marriage. Through the prism of personal experience and the countless lives I've guided as a confidante, I gleaned profound insights into the intricate labyrinth of relationships, particularly the delicate choreography of marriage. Despite lacking formal training in counseling or psychology, my gift lay in the ability to listen — to capture the whispers beneath the words, to probe, and to gently guide individuals to unearth their own blind spots, revealing paths of enlightenment that would aid in healing their relationships.

In the many counseling sessions I conducted, several patterns clearly emerged. In most relationships, across the spectrum of race, socio-economic profiles, class, or native heritage, a dual curse became evident: selfishness and ignorance. The ignorance of one's own value system and the ensuing selfishness born from it formed an insidious dyad that threatened the sustainability of the time-honored institution of marriage. I discovered that individuals often stepped into this sacred intersection of disparate lives, cultures, and expectations without the slightest inkling of their true selves or their purpose in existence. They ordinarily possessed no genuine comprehension of their emotions or the mental paradigms through which they negotiated life.

In many cases, the shackles of childhood wounds and unresolved emotional trauma often rendered them robotic automatons, practically devoid of the healing power of introspection and forgiveness. These burdens, unrecognized and unattended, morphed into invisible baggage packed with deep-seated prejudices, latent anger, a thirst for revenge, and suppressed frustration. Consequently, they unconsciously projected their anguish onto others in a fruitless and harmful bid to compensate for the harm inflicted on them by parents, loved ones, society, or friends. Even when they recognized their issues, an entrenched resistance or incapacity to address them prevailed. The outcome was an extended period of suffering, bitterness, and painful alienation from those they hold dear. As Fr. Richard Rohr, a renowned Catholic Priest, once sagely expressed, "If we do not transform our pain, we will most assuredly transmit it." My observations endorsed his wisdom.

During my tenure as a facilitator in the Catholic Archdiocese of Nassau's marriage preparation program, I aimed to steer participants through a journey of self-discovery. I prompted them to delve into the expanse of their existence, seeking answers to probing questions: Who are you? Where do you come from? Why are you here (on earth)? How did you arrive here? What are your conceptions of marriage and how do they align with the Church's teachings? Are you truly prepared for this pivotal vocation? What is your intended spouse's understanding of marriage? What daily practices do you now undertake to uncover the real 'you'?

The objective was to help them comprehend that communication is more than an exchange of words, ideas, or concepts, but, rather, a reflection of one's identity, worldview, attitudes, aspirations, and deepest wounds. The intent was to help them peel away the layers of their personalities and journey deep into the core of their being. Through this, I hoped to induce a profound introspection, a surprising yet enlightening revelation for many. Even those on their second or third marital journey had scarcely fathomed the true essence of marriage, particularly in light of the Church's teachings.

The self beneath the masks we wear, beneath the pretenses and ego-crafted caricatures, remains a stranger even to us. It hides behind countless facades, neatly woven since birth to curry societal favor or shield us from pain. Marriage, if lived authentically, could serve as a revealing mirror, exposing the true self beneath the games we play. Yet, most individuals continue to masquerade behind their false selves, avoiding the excruciating honesty that a successful relationship necessitates. Little wonder, then, that about half of all first-time marriages end in divorce, with a significant portion of the surviving half suffering a cauldron of conflict, selfishness, petty disputes, power struggles, and a dismal charade of authenticity. Statistics reveal a similar fate for second and third marriages. The ultimate casualty is the family, especially children, who are left to perpetuate the cyclical dance of dysfunction into their own futures.

The ego, after all, is a master of disguise, sparing no effort to avoid detection. Yet it cannot hide from the invasive scrutiny that time-tested practices like contemplation, meditation, affirmative prayer, mentoring, selfless service, and journaling afford. I knew that these practices, when applied diligently, could unearth its deceits. Therefore, it will go to great lengths to ensure its falsehoods remain undiscovered.

The marriage course wasn't the only platform where I shared these life philosophies. I was also a member of the media, a stage that I utilized to maximum value. The understanding I'd gleaned from my own experiences and those of the many couples I'd counseled was a wellspring of wisdom I shared. In many ways, these experiences transformed me, shaping my perspective on relationships, self-discovery, and the human condition.

I sought to touch the lives of those on similar paths, inviting them to look within, dissolve the coatings of their personalities, and arrive at a place of understanding and authenticity. I believed in the power of honest self-assessment to transform oneself, and relationships, and I wanted to offer those invaluable tools through all means at my disposal, media included.

In all these various iterations of my life, I saw myself as a catalyst for change, to break the cycle of dysfunction, and to help people build healthier, more fulfilling relationships rooted in mutual respect, understanding, and love. Thus, I continued on this journey, sharing and learning in equal measure, fueled by the belief in the transformative power of self-awareness and authenticity.

PUBLIC PERSONA & COMMITMENTS

Chapter Eighteen

Media

Throughout the PLP's initial quarter-century reign, Bahamians often bemoaned the monopolistic effects of the nation's radio and television airwaves. ZNS Radio and TV stood as the sole legal broadcast institutions of the era. This stifling of public broadcast communication was a ceaseless source of frustration for the Bahamian populace, yearning for diverse voices and perspectives.

In a published article of September 20th, 2006, titled 'Reforming Bahamian Broadcasting,' the late columnist Larry Smith vocalized this frustration when he highlighted the exclusion of Bahamian musicians whose lyrical content didn't meet the PLP's approval, the arbitrary business practices, the juvenile propaganda cloaked as evening news, and the habitual airing of "Roots" during election periods.[1] Smith's words painted a vivid picture of the Bahamian people's mounting impatience with the PLP's broadcast stranglehold.

Under the leadership of ex-PLP Cabinet Minister Hubert Ingraham, the then-opposition FNM made the bold promise to break the chains of broadcast restriction if elected in August 1992, —a promise they kept.

Within two years of the FNM's ascension to political power, a gifted opportunity sprang upon me. My former ZNS colleague, Wendall Jones, was granted a radio license by the new government. Seizing the moment, he immediately hired me as News Director and Talk Show host. Despite my modest media background—only a 5-month stint at ZNS in 1974 where Wendall and I worked as news reporters—I eagerly embraced this exciting possibility. The fact is, while at ZNS, I never had the chance to fully exploit my journalistic capabilities, a condition that I expected to change considerably with this new opportunity. Because of my full-time responsibilities as the Bahamas' Manager for Colgate Palmolive, New York, at the time, I was only able to supervise the newsroom for the production of the 7 p.m. daily newscast while hosting the Monday night talk show, "*Face-Off.*"

The FNM's liberation of the airwaves sparked an explosion of talk shows, an emblem of the newfound broadcast freedom. Wendall and I designed a platform for Bahamians to share their candid thoughts on a myriad of topics, predominantly the nation's political landscape. We swiftly formatted our radio programs to feature daytime and evening shows—"*Issues of the Day*" and "*Face-Off,*" respectively—alongside Wendall's pre-recorded "*Jones & Co*" on Sundays.

Excitement for talk radio was breathtaking. Talk shows, particularly those on the popular Love 97 Radio, attracted compelling, riveting attention from thousands of Bahamians. Journalist hosts like Wendall, Darold Miller, and myself introduced a style of respectful confrontation, injecting an investigative edge to discourses. The shows also served as a temperature gauge of the population's sentiment towards the government's performance. Government operatives often used the shows as a testing ground to assess the public response to certain proposals. Thus, talk shows became a reliable barometer of public opinion, informing the government to either proceed with or abandon initiatives.

With this expanded media presence, I became a household name. The benefits and burdens of fame also came along with it. Despite the privileged treatment and unique opportunities, I found the loss of privacy unnerving, particularly when in public with my family. The invasiveness was disconcerting, as was the occasional spread of false, hurtful, demeaning rumors. I strove to shield my family from the inevitable attacks, but the unfair treatment and expectations placed on them, simply because of my public profile, were difficult to understand, especially for my younger children.

Over time, my media career underwent several transitions—from hosting *"Face-Off"* to presenting *"Issues of the Day,"* to joining More 94's morning show, *"Real Talk Live."* My interest in morning programs was ignited after a visit to Jamaica, where such shows seemed popular. However, my stint with More 94 was brief. I then joined Guardian Radio in 2008 and remained until I entered front-line politics in November of 2016.

In addition to my radio commitments, I also hosted a variety of television shows including "*The Political View*" on Cable 12. As the title suggests, the show focused on political matters, with a revolving door of politicians and aspiring politicians as guests.

The talk-show culture that blossomed in the 1990s and continued into the new millennium fundamentally reshaped Bahamians' engagement with current affairs. While politics invariably dominated the daily chatter, a host of other critical subjects found their way into the conversation. Topics like education, the economy, crime, and the socialization of Bahamian youth—particularly males—gained significant attention.

The new era of unrestricted broadcasting did more than simply offer a platform for discussion; it became a mirror reflecting the nation's hopes, concerns, and aspirations. Every broadcast echoed the rhythm of the Bahamian heartbeat, uniting us in our shared desire for progress and our collective pursuit of a better future.

My media career spanned a period that corresponded with the evolution of Bahamian society and our collective struggle for greater expression, transparency, and democratic engagement. In many ways, that career path emulated the larger narrative of Bahamian broadcasting—from stifling control to the yearning for change, the promise of freedom, and concluding with the eventual flourishing of open-air dialogue. From this perspective, my story isn't just about personal fame or the challenges of public scrutiny. It's a testament to our collective will, our shared hopes, and our unending pursuit of a more inclusive, vibrant, and democratic Bahamas.

---

1. The TRIBUNE: Smith, Larry, Bahamas Pundit: September 20, 2006: Reforming Bahamian Broadcasting

Media Career

Talk show Host on "Jeffrey'"

Star 106.5

Chapter Nineteen

Diaconate

Shortly after Mass at St. Bede's Catholic Church one Sunday morning in 1993, Father Reginald Demeritte, Pastor, posed a question that left me slightly bewildered. 'You aren't considering the Deacon program?' he asked. A smile tugged at the corners of my mouth as I shook my head. 'No, Father,' I replied, gently reminding him of the turmoil at home. I was surprised that he didn't remember the serious health challenges Bern suffered at the time. Despite her usual radiant spirit, she was embroiled in a grim battle with a mysterious illness. At the same time, we were also raising two beautiful children, their youth and innocence a stark contrast to the gravity of our situation.

Truthfully, the notion of enrolling in the Diaconate hadn't graced my mind. I was already consumed by a myriad of Church activities, serving as Chairman of the Diocesan Bazaar Committee, President of St. Francis' Parish Council, parish commentator, and lector, among other roles. The thought of adding more to this already demanding repertoire was overwhelming. Yet, service, a concept deeply embedded in my psyche, was not instilled by external influences. It was an inherent part of me, as natural as breathing. It was this characteristic of selflessness that made me a favored choice for leadership roles.

I was privileged to become a member of the Rotary Club of Nassau, thanks to my cherished friend, Tony Wallas. Eventually, I ascended to the position of president, receiving the prestigious Paul Harris Fellow award twice for my devotion to service. However, the diaconate call returned a few years later, in 1995, with Bern, despite her health challenges, insisting that I was meant to serve the divine.

After an extensive interview process, I was selected in September 1996, with twelve other candidates for a four-year discernment to test our diaconal vocation. Guided by Sisters Eileen Kelly, SC, and Jacinta Neely, OSB, and Father Patrick Holmes, we scoured the domains of Scripture, Theology, Ministry, and Spirituality in one weekend per month at the Emmaus pastoral Centre, Fox Hill.

In the hierarchy of the Catholic Church, the Pope, cardinals, bishops, priests, and then deacons weave a pattern of faith and ordained service. Permanent deacons, either single or married, do not aim to become priests. Their duties include preaching, officiating at weddings, baptisms, and funerals, pastoral care, teaching the faith, counseling, and more. The permanent deacon shares his journey with his spouse. That is why the Church required both the candidate and spouse to attend the monthly classes to ensure mutual growth in faith.

On June 21, 2000, after an arduous four-year voyage, four of us were ordained as permanent deacons. I was assigned to my home parish, St. Francis Xavier Cathedral, under the guidance of Monsignor Simeon Roberts. Soon, my preaching, which mimicked the intellectual style and stimulation of Protestant sermons, started to impact the congregation significantly. In addition to my preaching duties, I was also assigned to conduct the Parish's adult catechetical program, known as Catholic Heritage. Because of my previous training in various spiritual traditions and disciplines, I came, over time, to understand and appreciate the different levels of spiritual development. This greatly served as a compass for my compassion, for myself, and for others. It gave me hope. This clarity was further refined when I led the weekly Catholic Heritage Program.

While the Heritage program was primarily designed to enlighten participants about the history, theology, and traditions of their faith, I selected a different pathway. In addition to an intellectual appreciation of their faith, I also recognized that parishioners longed for a more authentic experience of God through spiritual exercises, like meditation, contemplation, and selfless service.

My teaching drew inspiration from spiritual luminaries like Fr. Richard Rohr, who eloquently expressed the struggle of modern culture. He noted how people often missed the deep inner life and experience of their true selves in God. Similarly, the teachings of the late Fr. Thomas Merton were deeply anchored in my spirit. He emphasized the need to keep one's soul open, trusting in God and His grace to guide us forward when we are ready.

I realized that our consciousness evolves towards ever deeper unity and wholeness, even though it may not be apparent in the short run, and progress is often marked by periods of setbacks and breakthroughs. Yet, I remained hopeful and convinced that we were collectively moving towards a more conscious and unified existence. That conviction never left.

Deaconate
2000

Receiving The Book of The Gospels
from Archbishop Lawrence A. Burke (late)

Reverend Deacon, Mr. Jeffrey L. Lloyd

Chapter Twenty

SERVOL

Concurrent with my diaconal pursuits, the universe beckoned me with yet other leadership and advisory assignments. In September 1995, the Catholic Board of Education, a respected body that governed Diocesan-operated schools, extended an invitation for me to join their ranks. It wasn't the first time that such an invitation found its way to my doorstep. But familial obligations made it difficult for me to accept before.

At the conclusion of one of our monthly meetings, the late Archbishop Burke cornered me with an idea. His aura was charismatic as he proposed, "I would like to challenge you." I was taken aback, my facial expression probably mirroring my surprise and caution. He began to detail a youth development program in Trinidad, when his voice waned as if lost in a sudden stream of thought before he pressed on.

"Are you busy tomorrow?" he asked, his gaze now laser-focused. The question hung in the air, unanswered, as he swiftly moved on to his proposal for a discussion in his office.

This wasn't the first time the Archbishop had presented this idea to me. I previously dismissed it without a second thought, because the idea of working with young men, grappling with social dysfunction and academic challenges, wasn't enticing to me. My years as a teacher were behind me, I thought, and despite being unemployed at the time, I harbored no desire to return to the education sector, especially to engage with the troubled youth he proposed we serve. However, I held my tongue in the Archbishop's presence, my thoughts locked away.

Though apprehensive, I, nevertheless, found myself in his office the next day, joined by Monsignor Moss and Mrs. Renee Knowles, the Diocesan Financial Officer. I surmised that they were there as the Archbishop's reinforcements, to help persuade me to embrace this opportunity. Though somewhat hesitant, I decided to give it a shot. We outlined the plans for the four-month training in Port-of-Spain, Trinidad, the following January.

Lawrence Burke, a Jamaican Jesuit priest and Superior of the Jesuit Order in Jamaica, was anointed Bishop of the Catholic Diocese of Nassau, Bahamas, on July 17, 1981, and was consecrated on October 11, 1981. He served the Diocese devotedly for 18 years before being appointed in June 1999 as the Archbishop of the newly established Archdiocese of Nassau. In 2004, Pope John Paul II reassigned him to his hometown, Kingston,

Jamaica, to become the Archbishop of the Kingston Archdiocese. He retired in April 2008 and succumbed to cancer in Kingston in January 2010, at the age of 77. He was a beacon of hope, perpetually seeking to uplift those who had fallen on hard times. His endeavors spanned from supporting marginalized migrants to providing financial aid for aspiring college students and advocating for improved prison conditions. I was also on the end of his munificence when he provided a generous financial contribution towards Bernadette's medical expenses.

He sought to rejuvenate the lives of marginalized individuals trapped in a web of deprivation, tarnished self-esteem, and a dangerous lack of self-worth. This cycle often condemned many to a lifetime of despair, failure, and violence. I saw in him a man of incredible faith, such as on the ride home from a visit to the Office of then Prime Minister Hubert Ingraham, Christmas Eve, 1996. Archbishop confessed to me that while he didn't have the funds or resources to launch the proposed program, he was 'stepping out in faith', holding onto the staunch belief that we would find success somehow. This made a powerful impression on me.

He had a profound impact on me. His leadership style was inspiring; his tenacity in pursuing his objectives, his fearless candor, and humility, captured my imagination. He was visionary, fearless, faithful, and eternally optimistic. We developed a genuine bond as I, too, was not apprehensive about expressing my views, regardless of the audience. He appreciated this trait, often stating that he had no desire for sycophants in his circle but rather valued being challenged to confront his blind spots, and limitations, and to explore alternative perspectives on matters at hand. He appreciated my respectful candor and did not hesitate to voice his appreciation.

As a result of our mutual respect and shared values, he invited me to assume a more significant role in the leadership of the Diocese, beginning with an appointment in 1987 as co-leader of the Lay Leadership Development Program on evangelization, spearheaded by Professor Vincent Smiles. Subsequently, he assigned me to the Catholic Board of Education and later appointed me to two consecutive terms as Chair of the Archdiocesan Pastoral Council - a group of leaders tasked with advising him.

I arrived in Trinidad in early January 1997, only to be greeted by a culture shock. What I considered basic amenities back home were luxuries in my new environment. On my arrival, I was confronted with a water workers' strike, leaving me to collect water for hygiene purposes. The hardship spurred a sudden desire to retreat, but my commitment held me back. After enduring two weeks of water scarcity, I questioned whether I wanted to give this venture a fair shot.

My Trinidadian odyssey unfurled an intriguing encounter with SERVOL (Service Volunteered for All), an empowering tool for community development I never heard of before the meeting with Archbishop Burke in 1996. The enlightening discourses with SERVOL's Founder, Roman Catholic Priest, Father Gerry Pantin, and Sister Ruth Montrichard, Executive Director, painted a vivid portrait of its origins, mission, and overarching ethos.

This charismatic duo narrated an epoch fraught with social tumult, in Trinidad and Tobago during the late 1960s and early 1970s, during which citizens of the lower socio-economic stratum grappled with a pervasive sense of exploitation, disrespect, and alienation, exacted by a predominantly white, foreign oligarchy. This ruling class systematically excluded them from the bountiful fruits their society had to offer.

The simmering discontent climaxed in February 1970, when those residents, hailing primarily from the impoverished Laventille neighborhood, organized demonstrations in downtown Port-of-Spain, protesting the social and economic conditions they endured. These escalating protests, reverberating with the ethos of the "Black Power" movement, eventually burgeoned into a revolt, led by a faction of the highly trained Army, intending to topple the government.

According to SERVOL's records, the civil disturbances arrested the attention of Father Pantin, then a science educator at the prestigious St. Mary's College—an institution that ironically stood as a symbol of societal disparity—which forced him to question his vocational mandate. He was deeply affected by what he witnessed.[1] Peering through his classroom window at the throng of protesters, he realized that none of his students was amongst them – igniting a profound conviction that he was educating the wrong demographic.

Fr. Pantin promptly sought permission from his Superior to relinquish his teaching responsibilities and extend his assistance to the otherwise disenfranchised youth he saw on the streets. After an initial hesitation, he was eventually allowed to launch his humanitarian endeavor. However, his early ventures into the Laventille neighborhood were met with hostility and derision, as the residents accused him of attempting to 'save face'.

Unyielding in his resolve, he enlisted the aid of Wesley Hall, a famed West Indian cricketer then in Trinidad for a coaching stint with the West Indian Tobacco Company. Hall's presence somewhat quelled the locals' suspicions, gradually allowing the duo to establish constructive dialogues with various groups, marking the inception of SERVOL.

In time, Hall returned to his native Barbados, prompting Fr. Pantin to seek the aid of the Trinidad and Tobago Defence Force. Twelve soldiers and sailors were assigned to bolster SERVOL's nascent operations. Although bereft of knowledge regarding community development at the time, the team of Fr. Pantin and Officers adopted a refreshingly humble approach, continually asking each group, "How can we help you?"—a mantra that remains the organization's modus operandi. Father envisioned SERVOL as a platform to empower the underprivileged with the requisite skills to uplift themselves.[2] This, he told me, was integral to circumventing the culture of dependency and entitlement which many had suffered.

Understanding the community's needs meant conducting in-depth research and ongoing dialogue. The findings underpinned SERVOL's programs, tailored to the unique circumstances of each community. The goal was to empower the citizens to lead in their own development, thereby promoting a sense of ownership and responsibility.

SERVOL initially focused on vocational training in fields like mechanics, carpentry, masonry, and sewing. Gradually, the scope expanded to incorporate life skills training, addressing areas like self-esteem, anger management, and interpersonal communication. The organization adopted a philosophy of holistic development, which went beyond mere academic or vocational proficiency. Each participant was viewed as a special individual with unique needs and aspirations. This humanistic approach, combined with a strong emphasis on community engagement, was instrumental in breaking down barriers and fostering a sense of mutual respect and trust.[3]

It was particularly striking to see how SERVOL's programs evolved in response to changing societal needs. For example, in the 1980s, when Trinidad and Tobago experienced an oil boom, SERVOL expanded its vocational training to include areas like welding and electrical engineering. Similarly, in response to the AIDS epidemic that gripped the region in the 1990s, SERVOL launched health education and prevention programs that not only disseminated information about the disease but also facilitated discussions around taboo topics like sex and sexuality, promoting open dialogue and understanding.

Over the years, SERVOL impacted many lives, especially participants who were once marginalized and overlooked. Many not only gained employment but established their own businesses, becoming role models for future generations.

It was inspiring to see the ripple effect of SERVOL's work. Families were strengthened, communities revitalized, and a whole society benefitted. What began as an effort to address a local issue became a model of community development that was replicated in other parts of the world.

SERVOL showed me the transfigurational power of a daring vision and selfless service. Its work underscored the critical value of empowering individuals and communities to take charge of their development, demonstrating that sustainable change *was* possible when people were given the right skills and opportunity to use them. It was a lesson that inspired the Bahamas Catholic Church, led by Archbishop Burke, to inaugurate one of the most life-changing experiences for Bahamian youths that was ever conceived. And successfully implemented.

---

1. www.ServolTT.com

2. Ibid

3. Ibid

SERVOL
w. Fr. Gerry Pantin, Founder
1997

Chapter Twenty-One

The YEAST Rises

Returning home from Trinidad in April of 1997, I immediately set about creating a local incarnation of the SERVOL program. The name YEAST was proposed by Archbishop Burke, originating from the scripture verse Matthew 13:33: "The kingdom of heaven is like *yeast* that a woman took and mixed into about sixty pounds of flour until it worked all through the dough." Thus, was born the Youth Empowerment & Skills Training Institute or simply YEAST. Our guiding principle was drawn from SERVOL's motto: "committed to helping ordinary, imperfect, hope-drained people become agents of attitudinal and social change in a journey which leads to total human development."

Joining me in this venture were my inaugural staff, Mrs. Agatha Cartwright as Program Director, Mrs. Joye Ritchie-Greene as Assistant Director, and Mr. Tony Barnett as Vocational Director. Together, we envisioned an alternative educational institution that would cultivate self-assured, empowered individuals capable of leading their families and communities toward the realization of their full potential. Our hope was that our graduates would reduce the intractable unemployment rates, particularly amongst unskilled, uninspired, and vulnerable young men.

The program initially targeted disadvantaged, low-skilled, unmotivated adolescent males, aged 16-19, who had either deserted or been deserted by the formal education system, and were at risk of succumbing to a life dominated by crime, drugs, or violence. By the fall of 1997, The Bahamas was in the throes of escalating violence that imperiled the peaceful existence we had cherished. Rampant crime, a poor work ethic, and a culture of woeful underachievement posed a significant risk to the moral, social, and economic fabric of society. Just like the Trinidadian Catholic Church through Father Gerry Pantin, The Bahamas' Catholic Church felt compelled to act. Its objective was to restore respect for law, order, and human life, and equip present and future generations of Bahamians with the ability to compete on the global stage.

Much like our Caribbean counterparts, The Bahamas lacked a formal, recognizable period for young men to make the spiritual and psychological transition from boyhood to manhood. This usually led to a gaping void in their understanding of manhood since the models they observed were far from ideal. Consequently, their yearning for acceptance, positive guidance, and affirmation were often misinterpreted, and, too often, manifested in various forms of violence, disruption, aimlessness, truancy, and destruction.

When the FNM became the government in August 1992, it ordered an examination of the plight of the Bahamian youth, by commissioning a Consultative Committee on National Youth Development in 1993, chaired by former Anglican Archbishop, Rt Hon. Drexel Gomez. The Committee's mandate was "to study the special needs of young people and make specific recommendations for their positive development as an integral part of national planning."[1]

Two years later, the Committee issued a groundbreaking report, pointing out that, despite having free access, the Bahamian educational system had largely failed to equip students with marketable skills. The report suggested that this failure included a lack of preparation for students with an understanding of life issues, such as the natural environment, social responsibility, moral duty, and cultural heritage, which contributed to the aimlessness and uncertainty many had about their identity.[2]

The Committee strongly advocated broadening the educational curriculum from the primary level upwards to better prepare students for the working world. It recommended the inclusion of computer studies and a revamped syllabus for vocational and technical training to decrease the number of graduates lacking marketable skills.

The report also underscored the need to reduce the growing incidence of crime and violence in the community by the government and societal groups working together to engage disenfranchised youth. It suggested that this could be accomplished by the establishment of dedicated job placement and training programs, including job readiness training. This was to ensure that these individuals received the necessary support to join the workforce.

The Committee's report was a sobering acknowledgment that an increasing number of disillusioned youngsters had either become social, academic, or employment drop-outs. It warned that: "unless measures are taken to reach out to these young men, equipping them with essential life skills and vocational training, the number of at-risk youth opting for a life of crime, drugs, and self-destruction will continue to rise at an alarming rate year after year."[3] Additionally, the report blamed the insidious drug trade of the late 70s and early 80s as producing an increasing number of social misfits, which, in turn, triggered tragic cycles of incompetence, violence, aimlessness, deficient ethics, and despair, particularly amongst adolescent males aged 16-30 years.

In the face of such stark findings, Archbishop Burke felt that the Church was morally obliged to intervene. An alternative educational framework, especially for young men, seemed to be the most viable solution. Like Fr. Pantin, he understood that respectful, yet urgent interventions were needed to rescue 'unattached' Bahamian young men.

To some social commentators, the Committee's report was no surprise. They noted that the Bahamas had begun experiencing a social decline since the early 1970's, beginning in 1974, when the number of recorded births to unmarried women outnumbered, for the first time in Bahamian history, those born to married women. Among these respected observers was the Bahamian journalist, Nicki Kelly, who, in a Christian Science Monitor article of June 30th, 1981, described a country ensnared in a drug culture not of its own making. She quoted the former Attorney General, the late Paul L. Adderley, saying, "What we have is an extremely serious national problem. People at all levels have become engaged in a wide cross-section of criminal and corrupt activities that threaten to destroy our society."[4]

Ms. Kelly surmised that high unemployment and the election violence of 1968 and 1972 were partly responsible for the breakdown in law and order. However, she argued that the principal factor was the multibillion-dollar drug trade, which encouraged crime and corruption. The same inducements, she noted, that made the Bahamas successful as a tourism and banking center also proved attractive to drug merchants.[5] The Bahamas' unique geographical location, with its 700 islands and cays straddling some of the Western Hemisphere's most important shipping lanes, was an ideal drug route to the United States. The nation's secluded coves and beaches scattered across 100,000 square miles of water facilitated the hiding of drugs en route northward from Bolivia, Peru, Ecuador, and Colombia.

Ms. Kelly's article noted that by 1981, a number of Bahamians had increasingly become involved in the drug trade. For instance, by 1980, a staggering 64 percent of the 1,024 individuals charged with drug offenses before the courts were Bahamians. Quick profits from the drug trade were exerting tremendous social pressure, especially when one saw their neighbors getting rich overnight. The swift influx of illicit money presented an almost irresistible temptation to many.[6] This ill-gotten wealth allowed many to circumvent the law. When law enforcement officers attempted to investigate the drug trade in the islands, they encountered not just resistance but overt obstruction from local residents who promised retaliation for any who aided the investigating authorities, highlighting the entrenched fear within the community.

Kelly's potent narrative outlined that by 1981, the proceeds from drug smuggling had seeped into every corner of the Bahamian economy. She wrote of how drug money had become the lifeblood of many settlements, which were previously neglected by the government. In these forgotten corners of the Bahamas, drug money was seen not as the product of criminal activities but rather as the key to survival.[7]

It was against this backdrop that YEAST was launched. The urgent call to action was clear: at-risk youths needed not just academic and vocational training, but also guidance in moral and ethical responsibility. In the face of these societal challenges, YEAST's mission was clear: instill within these young men a sense of purpose, self-confidence, an understanding and appreciation of their cultural heritage, and equip them with the skills necessary to lift themselves and their communities out of the mire of underachievement.

The repercussions of the drug trade proved to be even more calamitous. The consumption of marijuana, methaqualone, and cocaine escalated, affected even the schools, and led to cases of children as young as seven being hospitalized for drug-induced psychoses. As Ms. Kelly's piece highlighted, by the early 1980s, Bahamian medical experts were adamant that drug abuse had morphed into the most dire health issue the Bahamas faced, even surpassing alcohol consumption. At that time, the Bahamas had the third highest per capita alcohol consumption globally.[8]

A direct correlation between drug use and a surge in violent crimes was also noted by the Police. From 1977 to 1981, Police stats showed that robberies more than doubled. An astonishing 70% of all crimes committed in 1980 involved weapons, leading the police to report that "Crime was at an all-time high in the Bahamas."[9]

While New Providence may have been the epicenter of drug trafficking, the once tranquil family islands did not remain untouched by this scourge. Young family-islanders, who ordinarily pursued careers in fishing or farming, were instead lured into the drug trade, or "fishing for drugs" as one contemporary writer put it.

There was no denying that the Bahamas, with a population of roughly 215,000 residents then, lacked both the human and financial wherewithal to combat the gargantuan problem. According to available statistics, the 1982 Bahamas Police Force comprised 1,218 personnel, a 13% decline from its strength in 1973. This was despite the fact that the crime rate had already doubled by 1981.[10] The government then conceded that they needed at least 500 additional recruits to address the rising crime levels. Nonetheless, this acknowledgment did not stem the avalanche of persistent criticism leveled at the force. There were allegations that major international and local drug traffickers operated with impunity in the

Bahamas, shielded by influential Bahamians with high-level government connections.

In a shocking 1982 television report, investigative NBC television journalist Brian Ross implicated members of the PLP Government. His report noted that the smugglers were allowed to use the Bahamas as a transshipment point for drugs destined for the US and Canada. In light of his damning allegations, and the ensuing uproar that followed, the Government established in 1984, a Commission of Inquiry to probe into the drug trade and allegations of official corruption in the Bahamas. The Commission's Report unmasked some disconcerting realities, resulting in the resignation or dismissal of several government Cabinet Ministers.

Specialized Curriculum

As I stepped into my mission with YEAST, it soon became apparent that providing young men with vocational skills was not enough. Some had already been exposed to such trades in high school. The issue lay deeper. They harbored a latent resentment, resistance, and defiance. They misunderstood their place in the world, their responsibility towards their society, and their own ability to cultivate self-discipline. Many were captured by a seething suppressed anger, mainly towards an absent father, but also towards, in their view, a complicit mother. The Church's task, then, was not merely to shape them into competent craftsmen, but to inspire them to become happier, healthier, capable self-aware men, fathers, and leaders.

To prepare for my role at YEAST, I delved deeply into literature exploring the plight of men. Books like Fr. Richard Rohr's "Wild Man to Wise Man", and Dr. Myles Munroe's "Understanding the Purpose and Power of Men: God's Design for Male Identity" and "The Fatherhood Principle" were invaluable resources. These literary assets revealed that a large percentage of young men grew up fatherless. This absence cast long, dark shadows over their lives, making them prone to mental illness, academic failure, addiction to harmful substances, unproductive pastimes, lack of motivation, shorter lifespan, criminal behavior, and unemployment. Shocking statistics in 1997 about the inmate population at Her Majesty's Prison seem to support this claim, which showed that out of approximately 1,400 inmates there, fewer than 30 were female, affirming the severity of the problem.

Drawing inspiration from the SERVOL model, YEAST was launched on September 8, 1997, with twelve trainees and a four-part component curriculum:

The Personal Development Course (PDC): This 12-week program was the cornerstone of YEAST, which took the trainees on a path of self-discovery. They reviewed the history of their lives from inception to present, forcing them to give honest responses to: Who am I? Where did I come from? What's my purpose?? What influences shaped my life and my perception of it?

For many, this was a pivotal turning point, leading them to confront themselves and their circumstances honestly, possibly for the first time. The impact was deeply moving. Many were able to shed burdens of guilt, confusion, self-doubt, and hidden pain, by understanding their familial history and cultivating self-awareness, emotional intelligence, and positive attitudes.

Basic Skills Training (BST): This segment was incremental to the PDC where trainees were enrolled in job-oriented courses including carpentry, electrical installation, plumbing, and computer technology. The construction trades of carpentry, plumbing, and electrical installation were mandatory for all trainees, which proved immensely beneficial so that each could find employment with near certainty in the construction or related field.

Apprenticeship: In the final weeks of the Skills Training, trainees were assigned to various companies that had partnerships with YEAST This allowed them to sharpen their skills in real-world work scenarios, encouraging them to understand the ramifications of adult responsibilities, and providing them with an opportunity to secure permanent employment.

Parent Enrichment Program (PEP): Recognizing the vital role of parents in their children's development, we insisted on their participation in the program. Mirroring the PDC, this component required parents to partake in deep introspection and critical evaluation of their own life experiences, fostering a holistic familial transformation.

However, soon after YEAST began, I sensed that our best efforts did not yield the fruits we hoped, if at all. We did not realize the severity of the negative attitudes and disordered behavioral paradigms to which the young men were routinely subjected. Sadly, the 12-week PDC, though beneficial to some extent, was simply no match for the overpowering effects of the toxic atmosphere in which the trainees were enmeshed. In our view, they needed a more intensive and persistent diet of positive reinforcement to instill the discipline, character traits, leadership, and teamwork required.

I scoured my imagination to conceive of the prototype of character traits that a YEAST student should demonstrate. My mind was cast back to an occasion while visiting the US Embassy building in downtown Nassau, where I observed the profile of the US Marine Corps Guard stationed there. I was captivated by his disposition – a posture of commitment, focus, precision, and impeccable appearance. Having attended school with former members of the Corps, I understood that the products of the Corps were individuals trained to respond with conviction, courage, and decisiveness. Honor, courage, and commitment were the bedrock of their ethos, defining not only their actions but also their thought processes. Though it had been decades since I was in their company, the characteristics I observed in them never left me. To my mind, these were the traits that not only the YEAST trainees needed to exemplify, but especially qualities our society needed in its youth.

The local equivalent of the Corps in the Bahamas is The Royal Bahamas Defence Force (BDF). My former schoolmate, Commodore Davey Rolle, was its Commander. I was convinced that his insights could help us structure a program imbued with training and skill sets that the BDF utilized for its recruits. Moreover, I realized that to effect deep, lasting change, we needed to isolate the trainees at least for a time from the negative influences of their environment. Consequently, I proposed the idea of utilizing suitable facilities in one of our Family Islands, away from the distractions of Nassau, where trainees could immerse themselves in a new setting for an extended period.

Instituting a program of this magnitude and nature was a first for the Bahamas. However, it received unanimous support from YEAST's Board, the public, and even the principals of SERVOL, who were impressed by the evolution of their model in the Bahamas.

When contacted, Davey thrilled me with his enthusiastic response. He not only shared my vision but also recommended a similar proposal he had prepared, echoing the same concerns about our young generation. He promised the commitment of the BDF to whatever extent was needed.

The next step was to find a suitable location with the necessary infrastructure already in place. After some exploration, I discovered Camp Symonette in James Cistern, Eleuthera, operated by the Methodist Church, as an ideal choice. They conducted multiple camps each year, primarily during the summer, for both local and international youths. They were more than happy to accommodate.

Thus, in September 1999, YEAST launched the first Character & Leadership Development Camp (CLDC) of its kind in The Bahamas, which we dubbed "Boot Camp." The two-week pilot scheme that featured twenty trainees produced impressive results. The progress that we witnessed in those two weeks far surpassed any similar achievement by them in the 12-week PDC. Instantly, we knew we had found our remedy. It only needed to be refined, expanded, and resourced.

Despite this initial success, we knew that significant hurdles lay ahead. At the time, YEAST's limited accommodations at its original home, the former Hardecker Clinic on Deveaux Street in Nassau, restricted the number of trainees we could enroll. As a result, we were forced to turn away many eager applicants. This, then, motivated me to explore expansion opportunities because we were determined to alleviate the social distress among youths in the Bahamian society, but doing so required more resources – technical, financial, human, and material.

In my quest for further development, I approached the Inter-American Development Bank (IDB) in the spring of 1998. After some discussion and a careful review of YEAST's program, the Bank supplied Mr. Ray East, a retired United Nations business development specialist, who had previously worked with small businesses in the Caribbean and Latin America to provide a roadmap of how YEAST could reach more young people. Ray and I spent six months meticulously reviewing statistics, studying global best practices, and interviewing various business, educational, and social services leaders to formulate a long-term development program.

In the end, he produced a report outlining a clear vision and path for the future of YEAST. These included:

a. Cement the Character & Leadership Development Camp (CLDC), our Boot Camp, as a fundamental component of the curriculum.

b. Broaden the Technical Skills Curriculum to include auto mechanics, masonry, tiling, air conditioning, refrigeration, computer technology, and electronics—each carefully chosen to cater to market demands.

c. Establish an endowment program, to secure a lasting source of funding.

d. Formulate a rigorous instructor certification system, modeled after SERVOL's time-tested teacher-training program; AND

e. Expand the Parent Enrichment Program, to include more parents.

Like all great visions, these too needed resources, especially financial. To this end, we sought the recruitment of a development officer to secure funds while elevating the Institute's presence in the community. As the realities of our budget constraints dawned on us, this task fell onto my shoulders—adding to the existing load of my teaching and administrative responsibilities.

Undeterred, I plunged into the role, advocating for our cause to the government, business community, and various organizations. I pleaded for additional grants, technical assistance, material donations, and financial support. The nature of our work, and the tremendously beneficial effect it had, struck a chord among the aforementioned entities, and the outpouring of support was overwhelming. This allowed us to extend the Camp incrementally from two weeks in 1999 to eventually nine weeks in 2003. The long-term vision was for YEAST to evolve into a full-time residential, off-island school.

By 2003, our efforts had caught the attention of the government. The program was not just the talk of the town, but was being examined as a possible model for a segment of proposed national youth service. The service was not a new concept. Sir Lynden Pindling had proposed a national youth service decades earlier, drawing inspiration from the Israeli model and the US Peace Corps. However, his detractors dismissed it as 'Pindling's army', and the idea was buried.

When the PLP regained power in 2002, however, the idea of a youth service saw daylight again. I was invited to join the Ministry of Youth's Task Force led by Youth Director, Ms. Autherine Turnquest, to explore ways in which the concept could materialize. The Force crisscrossed the country holding town meetings and interviewing leaders from different walks of life. Emerging from these consultations was the idea that certain youths – particularly at-risk ones – needed a disciplined, residential environment so that more profound behavioral and attitudinal adjustments could be ensured. Owing to our successful Boot Camp, YEAST was chosen as the pilot for *this* element of the youth service.

Thus, in May 2005, The Bahamas Government formally contracted YEAST to conduct a year-round, residential Boot Camp in North Andros. By September of that year, some one hundred 16-19-year-old young males were enrolled in YEAST school in Barq, North Andros. It was not long after that initial cohort that parents, community leaders, and other concerned citizens pleaded with YEAST to extend its enrollment to include males between the ages of 12 and 15 years because they recognized that the same elements of social, academic, and attitudinal dysfunction had begun to creep into that demographic. With the concurrence of the Government and YEAST's board, the Institute's student population was expanded to include the desired grouping.

By 2008, the newly elected FNM government began an intensive review of the cost of the program, citing budget severe constraints brought on by the global financial crisis. It *was* a trying time for the Bahamas. The crisis caused nearly a six percent GDP loss. I understood the fiscal challenge and sympathized with the difficult position it had imposed upon the new Government. However, I invited the Government to be careful about scrapping a program that proved such an enormous benefit to a constituency desperately in need of positive intervention. I asked them to appreciate how unwise it was to pour large sums of money into policing and prison upgrades, while being unwilling to invest a mere fraction of that amount into challenged young people, many of whom, without the intervention YEAST, would spiral into a path of crime and violence.

My appeals fell largely on unresponsive ears. Though some Cabinet members agreed with my perspective, their interventions proved unpersuasive. As a result, the YEAST experiment sadly ended in July 1999. By the time it did, it had made an enviable positive impact in the lives of over 1,000 young men and their families. In its 13-year existence, it had grown to employ a robust team of twelve Defence Force Officers and forty additional support staff. By 2009, it had become the second-largest employer in North Andros, outpaced only by the Bahamian Government itself.

Its premature closure did not erase the impact of YEAST, which continues to reverberate across Bahmaina communities. The program's successful run, juxtaposed with the worsening social conditions in The Bahamas, has led many since to call for its revival. Unfortunately, no Government considered it worthwhile to revive it.

Reflecting on this journey, I am filled with mixed emotions. We achieved much, inspired many, and made a tangible difference. Yet, there is a sense of unfinished business. Our work was not meant to be a one-time fix; it was a model to be nurtured, replicated, and integrated into the national fabric. However, even amidst these reflections, the spirit of YEAST lives on, cultivating hope, resilience, and a relentless pursuit of positive transformation.

---

1. Bahamas Consultative Committee on National Youth Development Report, 1994

2. Ibid

3. Ibid

4. CHRISTIAN SCIENCE MONITOR, Nicki Kelly, June 30th, 1981

5. Ibid

6. Ibid

7. Ibid

8. Ibid

9. 1982 REPORT, Royal Bahamas Police Force

10. Griffith, Ivelaw L. (1996-7), "Illicit Arms Trafficking, Corruption, and Governance in the Caribbean", Dickinson Journal of International Law, p 494.

Keynote Speaker at 2005 Y.E.A.S.T. fundraiser
Sir Sidney Poitier

2004 Graduating Class Y.E.A.S.T.
James Cistern, Eleuthera, Bahamas

PUBLIC ADVOCACY
SPIRITUAL EVOLUTION

Chapter Twenty-Two

Law

By the mid-2000s, the prospect of the Bahamas joining the Caribbean Single Market and Economy (CSME) had become a topical discussion in the society. Many Bahamian citizens expressed deep concerns about joining the Market, because of its perceived impact on our way of life.

A St. Francis Xavier Cathedral's parishioner, Attorney Reginald "Reg" Lobosky, deceased, was an ardent critic of this contemplated move. During one mid-Sunday morning conversation, after Mass at the Cathedral, he spoke words that touched me deeply. "Deacon," he said, "if you don't have a high school diploma, get one. If you have that but lack a college degree, seek it. And if you're already a college graduate without a Master's degree, then strive for that. Because if we join the CSME, our goose is cooked."

That dialogue, punctuating the morning's quiet reverence, forced me to reflect on my own qualifications. By then, I had earned my Bachelor's degree in 1973 from Xavier University. The future Reg envisaged - one in which the Caribbean region would become a single trading bloc – could turn my qualifications into mere footnotes. The possibility of skilled workers from other Caribbean countries flooding our markets seemed all too real. The populations of Jamaica and Trinidad vastly outweighed that of The Bahamas, and I was well aware of the legions of highly qualified professionals and artisans in those nations who were underemployed and would readily seek greener pastures in our country that was already lacking sufficient depth of expertise in various fields.

Confronted by this prospect, I realized my safest bet would be to venture into a profession immune to layoffs. As I pondered this, a single idea shone like a piercing flashlight – Why not become a Lawyer? That very day, I plunged into my research, propelled by Reg's admonition, and the reality that was dawning on me. His wisdom had lit a path forward for me, one I had never previously considered.

Reg's life, marked by active political participation, legal accomplishment, and deep personal transformation, was proof of his ability to adapt and grow. It reminded me of the ever-evolving nature of life and our capacity for change, irrespective of where we start. I reminisced that as we sail through life, confronting the challenges, it is essential that we continually invest in our growth and education, to equip ourselves for the changing realities of human existence. This realization, born from that mid-Sunday conversation with Reg, was a witness to the fact that wisdom can be found in the most unexpected of places, and the searing impact that it can have on one's life path.

Legal Career

The Honourable Alfred Sears, King's Counsel (KC), and I shared a common history as students at SAC. I was always in awe of his sharp intellect and the soft charisma he exuded. My admiration for him soared to new heights when he established and spearheaded the International Youth Organization - a group devoted to kindling national awareness in the formative years of the 1970s. This organization was a powerhouse of vibrant, ardent, and patriotic youths, guided by Alfred's visionary leadership. Soon after the organization had started rippling through the Bahamian society, Alfred departed for further studies in New York, spending two decades there. During his visits home, we never missed an opportunity to reconnect, nurturing our deep-seated friendship and mutual respect.

In May 2002, he stepped into the political arena as an elected member of the House of Assembly for the Fort Charlotte constituency. In swift succession, he was appointed as the Attorney General and Minister of Education. In the infancy of his political appointments, we convened at his office on Shirley Street, where he urged me to pursue a legal career and join his legal team. For years before, this proposition existed as a nebulous thought, only to be stirred to clarity during my enlightening conversation with Reg.

With the idea of pursuing law now actively occupying my mind, the real catalyst to take the plunge came from my friend Halson Moultrie, who by then had also embarked on his legal education through a distance learning program. With that, my resolution solidified - I would become a lawyer. Uncertainty loomed over the financial aspects and the practicalities of integrating this endeavor with my substantial familial responsibilities, but I was committed to venture forth. Hence, in January 2004, I began my legal studies.

This pursuit turned out to be as metamorphic as it was formidable, causing seismic shifts in my thinking. The workload was much heavier than I anticipated. I quickly formed a study group with long-time friends Hallie, Edgar Moxey, Keith Seymour, and a few others. The group became an invaluable intellectual commune where we deciphered and simplified complex legal principles. The phrase "think like a lawyer" began to assume its definitive contours, guiding our group discussions. It was a phrase that meant more than mere logic, morality, or conventional understanding of truth. Rather, it demanded meticulous attention to detail, the ability to comprehend multiple meanings of words, contextual understanding, and the skill to formulate arguments for any stance.

I initially struggled with this idea, feeling that it eroded my convictions and principles, turning me into a mercenary of sorts. However, with time, I understood that learning to argue from multiple perspectives meant acknowledging the existence of valid counterpoints.

On October 26, 2009, members of our study group, among others, were called to the Bahamas Bar. My legal training heightened my existing abilities like sound judgment, argument analysis, empathic listening, and understanding contrasting viewpoints argued in good faith. It enabled me to sift through arguments by discarding illogical, inconsistent, frivolous, and harmful ones that reflected reprehensible values such as racism, human degradation, and greed.

True to his word, Alfred welcomed me as a member of his firm upon the completion of my formal legal training. He was kind and gracious in allowing me to work during the summer recesses while in Law School. As I pursued my career, I realized that "thinking like a lawyer" was essentially thinking like an enlightened human being - harmonizing passion and principle, reason and judgment, embodying tolerance, sophistication, pragmatism, and engagement. The voyage to becoming a lawyer reshaped me – developing in me a refined perspective on life and humanity.

Call to The Bahamas Bar
1999

Chapter Twenty-Three

Jaya One

THE SUMMER OF 2011 found me in the Office of Archbishop Patrick Pinder, contemplating my future as a Permanent Deacon. Our shared agreement concluded that my resignation from the Diaconate was the best course of action given my desire to remarry. He believed that my chances of remaining a Deacon, should I marry, were slim despite the Church's flexibility in certain circumstances. Notwithstanding this change, my determination remained fixed to continue guiding a group of interested seekers committed to studying and practicing spiritual disciplines, much like I did with the Catholic Heritage group.

The Archbishop's counsel was rooted in ecclesiastical rules. A 2017 article in the Southern Cross, a Catholic magazine based in South Africa, referenced a 1998 policy by the Vatican's Congregation for Divine Worship and the Discipline of the Sacraments that allowed certain exceptions for widowed deacons based on their usefulness to their diocese, or if they were left with young children or aging parents-in-law to care for.[1] In

2005, however, the rule was revised without explanation. Currently, only the Pope can grant a dispensation, provided the deacon's ministry is of significant value to the diocese and that he has young children to raise.

Deciding not to contest the matter, I accepted the Bishop's decision and proceeded forward. My choice to relinquish diaconal duties emerged after deep contemplation, prayer, fasting, and widespread consultations with my mentors and advisors. The path towards matrimony felt irrevocably right. Michelle Donna Marie Mitchell, whom I had known for many years, and whose life perspectives corresponded neatly with mine, entered my life in the fall of 2009, two full years after Bernadette's passing. She possessed the blessed feature of a commitment to her evolution and the willingness to facilitate that of others, especially mine.

I was certain of my commitment to this path, and my heart and soul joined in that assurance. I intended to be honest with and true to myself, having no inclination towards celibacy following the demise of my spouse, nor the urge for transient amorous escapades. I felt a profound call to spiritual actualization, which I intended to pursue passionately. I also aspired to share my spiritual understanding and knowledge with those similarly intrigued by this interest, fueling my desire to continue facilitating the group of avid seekers.

Despite suggestions from some in my circle to switch to Anglican or Methodist denominations, where clergy are allowed to remarry if widowed, my Catholic faith was unyielding. Though I have a profound respect for all faith traditions and have participated in many during my spiritual quest, I chose the catholic tradition as the primary religious expression of my earthly incarnation. God does not reside exclusively within the realm of any organized belief system, but rather, embodies, in pure democratic fashion, equal availability and presence to all. My spiritual practice, after all, was wide and diverse, including disciplines such as meditation, chanting, affirmative prayer, yoga, and selfless service.

I considered myself more a student of metaphysics and the new thought movement than an orthodox religious devotee, principally due to the divine awakening experience in November 1982, which irrevocably changed my life. Confined within the boundaries of orthodox religiosity, I wouldn't have ventured into vibrant explorations with New Thought thinkers such as Ernest Holmes, Michael Bernard Beckwith, eastern spiritual tradition Masters, Helen Blavatsky, and many more.

Thus, my commitment to continue my spiritual journey and share that acquired wisdom with others was non-negotiable. With the Diaconate behind me, a third marriage on the horizon, and a budding relationship with an ascended master, I reflected on ways to embody my calling for spiritual leadership and development. There was a definite need to continue growing spiritually and help others discover, their "deep truth," as author and spiritualist Greg Braden once stated

Epiphany

The morning's cascading water, within the confines of a shower, was usually the precinct in which my greatest revelations arrived. It was in this exact sanctuary of solace that numerous exercises for the Catholic Heritage, including a unique austerity program in 2005, were conceived. It was here, too, that I received flashes of insight into topics and ideas for retreats, sermons, and other spiritual undertakings. The shower was a fertile ground for creativity and innovation, a haven for my spiritual brainstorming.

During one such prescient moment, the idea of establishing a mystery school surfaced, reminiscent of the ancient institutions where spiritual life was taught. It became clear that the focus of this school should be the I AM Consciousness, with me serving as a guide for others on the journey to the I AM, the Self, rather than assuming the role of a Teacher, Reverend, or Master. Although I possessed the 'indelible' seal of Holy Orders, through my Diaconate ordination, I no longer practiced in that role. Thus, the title of Reverend was not even under consideration. On Wednesday, January 25th, 2012, I conducted the inaugural session of the 'mystery school', under the jurisdiction of The JayaOne Institute of Mystical Studies.

My initial encounter with the concept of a mystery school came through my involvement in Eastern spiritual traditions. There, I learned about the Gurukula, or School of the Master, where seekers, eager to experience and comprehend the mysteries of God-consciousness, submitted to the guidance, discipline, and training of a Realized Master. Unlike traditional religions, which spoke *to* the existence of a supreme being, mystery schools delved into the realm of mysticism, enabling seekers to have *an experience* of the divine, in pursuit of union with God or the Absolute. Modern parallels of this are found in ashrams or monasteries, where a guru, abbot, abbess, or living master helps to steer the seeker's journey toward self-realization.

Until recently, mystery schools operated in secrecy, potentially because their teachings held the deepest understanding of life, entrenched in ancient shamanic wisdom and paths of enlightenment. It also may have been that their primary duty was to preserve the knowledge of the ancients and protect it from being carelessly divulged to aspirants who may not be ready to understand or appreciate its esoteric value. However it was, I was utterly captivated by this concept, drawn toward the sacred vocation of spiritual mastery. I yearned not just for academic knowledge but for 'gnosis', a term coined by the Greeks indicating a spiritual insight into humanity's true, divine nature. And so, with this yearning to understand and share this deep truth, my journey continued.

The Divine Principle: I AM

The I AM, a timeless concept, has donned many cloaks across various religious and spiritual doctrines. It's called Atma in Hinduism, God in Christianity, Allah in Islam, Jehovah in Judaism, Ground of Being by theologian Paul Tillich, and the Self in Eastern spiritual beliefs. Regardless of the nomenclature, the I AM is widely recognized as the primeval energy, the divine or cosmic consciousness, thus forming the foundation of all spirituality and religion.

In the modern era, scientific exploration began to verify what spiritual traditions had known for centuries: That the I AM is a dynamic, radiant, pure energy, teeming with potential and endowed with a vibrational potency that allows it to manifest in countless ways and forms; that this principle underpins every aspect of existence - from inanimate rocks and minerals to animate beings such as humans; from the smallest sub-atomic particles to the largest celestial bodies; from the oceans on our planet to galaxies far beyond our reach; that everything at its fundamental core is united, belonging to an inseparable unity of being. However, despite this universal oneness, humanity has persisted in perceiving the world through fragmented lenses. This sense of division was so deep-seated that it led to numerous religious wars, fuelled by the misconception of the superiority of one's belief over others.

As time progressed, I realized that the most formidable obstacle to embracing the fundamental truth of unity was the deep-rooted indoctrination by religious institutions. By attending numerous retreats and spiritual courses, I began to unravel the profound truth of the Oneness of all that is. It was a monumental leap of understanding for me - that I, and indeed all of us, are sparks of supreme consciousness, innately infused with the same divine qualities as Source/God. This realization still fills me with awe, deepening daily, and becoming more 'real' for me.

My ongoing spiritual journey helped me discern that much of my understanding of life was borrowed from others – whether society, parents, teachers, elders, or neighbors - and adopted without question or scrutiny. I failed to comprehend that these perspectives were the reflections of the individuals who held them. I didn't comprehend that they, like me, were also 'victims' of 'transmitted' information, handed on from the same sources that indoctrinated me. By adopting these views, I unknowingly subjected myself to the same inhibitions, biases, projections, doubts, fears, insecurities, and divisions that they held. In essence, I was merely repeating what I learned from others, oblivious to the truth of my own being, as the Self.

The Same Divine Essence: Different Labels

Monsignor (Msgr) Preston Moss introduced me to Father Richard Rohr, a Catholic Priest renowned for his transformational theology. In one of his books, Simplicity, Fr. Richard referenced the Vatican Council's affirmation of the unity of all peoples and their shared goal, God. This inclusivity and respect for other religions was enlightening, yet sadly, since its proclamation in 1965, there has been limited progress towards ecumenical unity, particularly within the Catholic Church. This deepening divide was unfortunately evident when a certain Pope once asserted that the Catholic Church was the "fullness of the repository of divine revelation". With such an arrogant claim, he overlooked the fact that the divine reality, God, is omnipresent, pervading every aspect of existence equally. Thus, God is as much in the Catholic Church as He/She/It is anywhere else.

The profound truth is that our true essence is identical to that of God, Jesus, Buddha, Mohandas Gandhi, the delicate butterfly that graces a lamppost, or the cosmic energy that engendered the Milky Way galaxy. The fundamental difference between us and figures like Jesus is their awareness of their oneness with God, as expressed by Jesus when he said, "The Father and I are One." The path to such enlightenment lies in the realization, as the late Fr. Thomas Merton penned in his seminal work New Seeds of Contemplation, that "this 'new man', spiritually and mystically one identity, is at once Christ and myself."

Like many others, I was raised to view myself as a sinful creature, separated eternally from God. I perceived the Bible as the inerrant word of God, delivered from heaven to the pious men and women of old. I was conditioned to believe that God was *only* revealed in the Christian tradition and nowhere else; that the adherents of other religious pathways were deemed lost or misguided; that their sacred texts were wrong, and concept of God was false. This led to the belief that the truth about God could only be accessed through faith in Jesus Christ, "the way, the truth, and the life."

While this nascent understanding of God might suffice for a child, whose universe is limited to their immediate surroundings, such a notion cannot hold water for the enlightened individual who recognizes the vast expanses of the universe. As my understanding and experiences matured through deep meditation and prayer, I came to see God as an unfathomable mystery, beyond the grasp of human comprehension, that deepens and expands with each dive into the reality we call God.

Repeating the sentiments of Father Richard Rohr in Simplicity, I accept that our spiritual journey usually begins with a conservative, almost possessive view of God. But as we evolve, we are required to outgrow this immature understanding and embrace the immenseness of the Divine.[2] As the late Bishop John Shelby Spong eloquently put it, "We walk into the mystery of God; (but) we do not define that mystery."

---

1. 2017 Southern Cross, South Africa

2. "Simplicity: The Freedom of Letting Go", Richard Rohr (2004).

Spiritual Director, JAYA.ONE
2003

Chapter Twenty-Four

Partisan Politics

Although I never felt an affinity towards the game of politics, my childhood was steeped in it. As mentioned earlier, my mother was an enthusiastic advocate of the Progressive Liberal Party (PLP), while my father harbored a secret loyalty to the United Bahamian Party (UBP).

To me, the word 'politics' evoked a grim portrait of underhanded and dishonest machinations. The mere thought stirred feelings of distaste in my spirit. I knew, instinctively, it wasn't the path for me. Yet, I was driven by a profound desire to make a meaningful difference in my country. I just didn't believe politics was the vessel for that ambition.

Growing up in Kemp Road, I wrestled with the community-imposed stereotype of low self-worth and an even lower sense of self-image. These barriers often stifled my genuine attempts at self-determination and belief in my own potential and capabilities. However, somewhere deep inside, the seeds of success were quietly sprouting. Without this silent growth, I would not have been the lighthouse of hope or the beam of possibility to countless individuals who sought my counsel, guidance, and wisdom over the years. Hope, that powerful force, was the thread woven into the fabric of my life. It was captured in the unfaltering words of encouragement spoken to me by teachers, neighbors, family, and especially my grandmother. It fanned the flames of this eternal craving. Even in the face of external adversity, I never relinquished the belief that something exceptional was on the horizon for me. The details of when, where and how were indistinct, but I held onto an intractable conviction nevertheless.

Hope propelled me through the entanglement of life's challenges. It bore a resemblance to the child-like dependence on something greater than myself, a belief in a divine plan unfolding beyond my control. It was a potent reminder that our lives are not the axis around which the world spins. Without hope, subtly hidden beneath the conscious surface of my thoughts, I would not have embarked on the journey I did: from becoming a well-rounded SAC student, to a beloved teacher; from starting my own business in New Orleans and the Bahamas, to creating an alternative school for at-risk young men, thereby transforming their lives for the better. Hope moved me to engineer one of the most successful Junkanoo seasons in the history of Bahamian culture and sustained my commitment to be a model husband and father. It inspired me to serve through the sacred avenue of the Diaconate, while helping to satiate the spiritual thirst of hundreds through my spiritual mentorship. Ultimately, it was hope that ruptured the portal of possibility to become a Member of Parliament and eventually appointed Cabinet Minister. None of these achievements would have been possible without the omnipresent flame of hope in my life, though, at times, it may have been momentarily dimmed by life's trials and tribulations.

One morning in early 2016, when a certain close friend arrived at my law office, I presumed he needed assistance with a legal matter. During a previous visit, he subtly probed my willingness to consider partisan politics. His underlying intentions came to light during our solemn Wednesday morning meeting when he invited me to help establish and possibly lead a new political party to challenge the existing political powerhouses. He didn't know of my quiet yet fervent disdain for partisan politics. Despite being intimately familiar with the political landscape as a journalist, and my camaraderie with many political figures, the merest contemplation of politics, as it was practiced in our region, incited a vehement abhorrence in my heart. I always admired and respected those who stepped up to the political plate - their bravery, tenacity, and personal sacrifices. Over time, I became privy to their silent lamentations and regrets, confessed in hushed tones after their lives had been consumed by the unforgiving game of politics which further deepened my respect and empathy for them. However, their experiences and countless others fortified my conviction that politics was not my destined path. Thus, my friend's proposal was summarily dismissed.

Unfazed by this initial rebuff, he returned several weeks later armed with the same proposal. Surprisingly, this time, not only did I lend him an ear, but found myself intrigued by his suggestion. Consequently,

I granted him the green light to investigate the feasibility of such a venture, an opportunity he seized with relish. Simultaneously, I initiated my own quest, seeking guidance from trusted friends and associates. While they unanimously acknowledged my capacity and qualifications to spearhead a fledgling political entity, all doubted its potential success since its formation was too close to an upcoming general election, and the acquisition of substantial resources, especially financial, that would have been necessary to mount a formidable challenge against the established parties, seemed a nearly unachievable objective. Their justification lay in the entry of The Democratic Alliance (DNA) that previously entered the political arena which, though performed admirably, served as a sobering reminder of such challenges. Despite capturing significant public interest, the DNA had twice failed to secure a single seat. Clearly, the task was far from straightforward. Nevertheless, I decided to undertake this exploratory venture. As predicted by some, the endeavor eventually sputtered out, but not before whetting my appetite for front-line politics, and opening my mind's door to other tangible possibilities.

Ratification

Since my return from college in 1974, I have been courted by various political parties at different junctures. They all tried to coax me into offering as a candidate, or at the very least, becoming actively involved.

For reasons I have previously stated, I routinely dismissed these overtures. However, the pressure to become actively involved escalated over the decades, in tandem with the growth of my public profile. The FNM was particularly persistent in seeking my endorsement. But, it wasn't a political figure who eventually swayed me, though.

"All this talent and intelligence, and all you're doing on the radio is criticizing and complaining, instead of stepping up and helping to fix the problems," a petite, young woman sharply asserted one day as our paths crossed in a parking lot near our offices, which were only a stone's throw apart. Her brusque tone and manner startled me, particularly since I knew her as a generally pleasant and obliging public servant. Struggling to regain my composure and respond, she threw down the gauntlet with a challenge, "Put up or shut up," before storming off.

I stood rooted to the spot, taken aback not just by her audacious approach, but also because she had managed to strike a chord deep within. I found myself wondering, "Am I indeed a coward? Why am I not utilizing my talents to accomplish meaningful differences? Wasn't making a contribution to society one of the primary reasons I had ventured into journalism in the first place?" This unexpected encounter sparked a series of introspective thoughts and queries that would not cease.

A fledgling conviction slowly began to crystallize in the corridors of my mind – an openness to the tantalizing possibility of becoming a political candidate. A whisper in the wind, perhaps the voice of God itself, seemed to beckon me toward a future framed in the arena of politics. As previously discussed, my friend, along with a cohort of like-minded individuals, undertook a daring exploration into the creation of a fourth political party. Embarking on this political expedition, they organized numerous meetings with intellectuals, potential candidates, prospective donors, and potential party members. The careful orchestration of this exploration was aided by consultants, helping them investigate the feasibility of such a venture. However, the harsh realities of time and financial constraints eventually resulted in its merciful dissolution.

One determined spirit, the then leader of the FNM, Hubert Minnis, refused to be deterred by my continuous rejections of his propositions. He remained unbowed, arranging numerous coffee and lunch meetings, and attempting to persuade me of the substantial impact I could have by offering as a political candidate. He painted a vivid vision of the FNM as an engine of transformation, propelling the Bahamas into the 21st century. His passionate conviction struck a chord within me, resonating with the mantra of 'transformation' that I had adopted over thirty years prior. Having witnessed first-hand the desperate need for a revolutionary overhaul of society through my experiences with YEAST and Baha Mar's Leadership Development Institute (LDI), I was convinced of the necessity for a radical, positive shift in our nation if we aspired to be a competitive force in the global marketplace of the 21st century.

In our final tête-à-tête, I placed two alternatives before him: Either continue leveraging the media to support the FNM or step forward as a candidate myself. He sought a night's grace to ponder my propositions.

However, I suspected the decision was instantaneous, for early the next morning, his verdict was declared: Candidate.

The option of utilizing the media to endorse a political position wasn't unfamiliar terrain for me; I had previously navigated these waters. Back in February 2002, in the months leading up to the general elections, the FNM government held a referendum where all proposals were rebuffed by the voters. In the aftermath, then-Prime Minister Hubert Ingraham was accused of politicizing the exercise and following the defeat, confessed to his "shame of the Bahamian people." The very next day, moved by his statement, I took to my LOVE 97 Show, Issues of the Day, vociferously demanding his resignation, asserting that: "If he is ashamed of us, we are ashamed of him. And he must resign forthwith. He doesn't deserve to be the PM of a people he is ashamed of." In subsequent broadcasts, I unreservedly urged the voters to dismiss Mr. Ingraham and the FNM in the 2002 general election, and instead, choose the PLP. The people *apparently* heeded my call.

In 2007, the winds of my support shifted. This time, revelations of corruption within the PLP Government and the Anna Nicole Smith affair besmirching the national dignity of the Bahamas, led me to publicly advocate for a vote in favor of the FNM. I postulated that Prime Minister Perry Christie had relinquished managerial control of his government, displaying tepid and indecisive leadership amidst a series of scandals. Once again, the people *seemed to have* heeded my call, electing as PM Hubert Ingraham whose resignation I had demanded a mere five years earlier.

Once I accepted the mantle of candidacy, I expressed my desire to represent the Marathon Constituency, where I once resided. However, the political stars were not aligned in my favor, as Marathon had already been pledged to another candidate. Consequently, I was presented with two alternatives: either represent a Family Island constituency or South Beach. South Beach, akin to Marathon, had also been promised to another candidate. Yet, Minnis expressed faith that the designated candidate might be persuaded to yield the ground in my favor.

In November 2016, I received the official endorsement from the General Council of the FNM, cementing my position as the standard-bearer for South Beach in the 2017 general election. At this point, I confess, my knowledge of party-level politics was embryonic. I had never taken part in an election campaign and humbly admitted the same in my inaugural meeting with the members of the South Beach Association. I invited them to guide me through the uncharted waters of election campaigning and, if successful, political representation. Among them were veterans of many political battles, and seasoned political campaigners. From the moment of my ratification, we knitted ourselves into a cohesive unit, tirelessly working to win the hearts and endorsement of the people of South Beach.

Our labours bore fruit on May 10th, 2017, as I was elected the Member of Parliament for South Beach in a resounding victory. On May 15th, I was appointed Minister of Education -- A moment of triumph that signified the culmination of a journey and the beginning of another, laden with the responsibility to serve my people and nation.

However, the vicissitudes of politics, much like the ebb and flow of the ocean tides, brought a wave of change on September 16, 2021. The FNM suffered defeat in the election, and I, in turn, lost my seat. Such is the landscape of politics, a terrain constantly reshaped by the winds of public sentiment. Yet, every end marks a new beginning, and every loss is a lesson from which to glean valuable wisdom.

Political Campaign
2017

Rev. Dr. Charles E. Rolle praying for FNM Candidate for South Bch Jeff Lloyd & His Wife

FNM Candidate for South Bch Jeff Lloyd at Mt. Nebo Baptist Church

Sworn in as Minister of Education by
Her Excellency, Dame Marguerite Pindling, ON GCMG
May 15, 2017

Presentation at UNESCO - PARIS
Minister of Education
November, 2019

Epilogue

LIFE'S LESSONS

Turning the page to the seventieth chapter of my life on October 6, 2021, conferred upon me a distinct privilege – a panoramic perspective of life's journey, painted with varied hues of experiences and lessons.

The milestone came at an intriguing juncture in my existence. The FNM and I had just tasted the bitter draught of defeat in an election we expected to win. The gavel of the public verdict left me unemployed, an outcome that led me to decide to take a much-needed sabbatical to rest, rejuvenate, reflect, and envision my future trajectory.

The concept of 'normalcy' is subjective. It is any condition that sustains, endures, and is pervasive. Although the cultural parlance of my youth stigmatized me as a 'bastard', I bear witness to life's bountiful blessings upon me.

A child blossoms best in a nurturing environment, imbued with support, encouragement, and safety. Yet, life often scripts a different narrative, normalizing the opposites if they are persistent and commonplace. I was blessed, for as a child, even though I was surrounded by neighbors whose lives often ricocheted between violence, deprivation, and chaos, their resilience and unwavering determination to overcome their circumstances served as my formative lessons. Many of my contemporaries deemed me underprivileged, lacking modern amenities such as indoor plumbing, electricity, phone connectivity, and vehicular transport. While they weren't entirely wrong, I was blissfully oblivious of these deficits at the time.

As I ventured further into life, I understood the essence of life is not about where you come *from*, but what you come *to.*

Throughout my journey, life has revealed some timeless principles that transcend social, racial, ethnic, economic, and religious boundaries. I share some here with You:

a. Observe Actions, Not Words

Following the 2011 by-election, I asked Cassius Stuart, then Leader of the Bahamas Democratic Movement (BDM), about the insights he had gleaned from his decade-long political journey. His reply was profound: "Don't mind what people say, watch what they do". He shared that despite people promising him their vote, their actions sang a different tune. This brought to mind the sayings of my youth: "Actions speak louder than words" and "Mouth could say anything", and even the words of Jesus in

Matthew 7: "Every good tree bears good fruit, but a bad tree bears bad fruit. A good tree cannot bear bad fruit, and a bad tree cannot bear good fruit."(KJV). I've learned that the actions people perform over and over again, not the words they speak, are the true proof of who they are.

b. *Educate Others On How to Treat You*

The way we present ourselves through words and actions sends a message to the world about our identity and how we should be treated. As a young teacher, I sought to uphold the respect and admiration society bestowed upon teachers. I committed to being honorable, respectable, and professional, never embarrassing myself or the teaching profession. This mindset manifested in how people addressed me. Even individuals significantly older than me always referred to me as "Mr. Lloyd". This, I believe, was not only the respect I extended to them, which was reciprocated, but the way I carried myself. The late Pastor Dr. Myles Munroe once said to me, "Dress how you wish to be addressed". This can also be adapted as: "Treat others as you wish to be treated."

c. *Mistakes Are Lessons*

I once heard Oprah Winfrey remark that she did not perceive her life's mistakes as failures but as lessons. This reframing was enlightening. Father Richard Rohr reinforced this idea, suggesting that success offers us little wisdom, whereas failure is a potent teacher. Our most enduring and meaningful lessons arise from mistakes and disappointments, not so much our victories. This principle holds true in my life as well.

The lessons I learned from my 'mistakes' far outweigh any insights I gleaned from my successes. The setbacks, disappointments, and failures were the most impactful events in my life. The person I am today, the wisdom I have, and the resilience I demonstrate are attributes that were largely shaped and tempered in the crucible of life's adversities.

d. Liberate Yourself Through The Grace of Forgiveness.

I spent a significant part of my life under the impression that forgiving another equated to absolving them of their wrongdoings, as though offering them a free pass. However, as I traversed the path of wisdom, I came to understand that forgiveness is, in fact, an act of self-empowerment. I saw how harboring feelings of anger, revenge, bitterness, or distress towards another depleted *me* of the vital life force I needed to envision and actualize my future. To live under the shadow of unforgiveness is to exist in the past, which ultimately controls one. Holding onto resentment is the misdirection of vital energy, which could otherwise be channeled towards personal growth.

e. Resistance is Futile, but Focus Fuels Expansion.

We often find ourselves in a constant state of resistance – against change, our problems, our circumstances, our peers, our responsibilities, and even our existence. Unbeknownst to many, such resistance serves only to exacerbate our issues. Carl Jung warned us that whatever we resist will not only persist but also grow larger.

f. The Journey Holds More Value Than the Destination.

We often become so engrossed in our goals, our picture-perfect outcomes, and the end result that we overlook the beauty of living in the moment and the joy of the journey. Pause, take a deep, cleanse the breath, and give yourself permission to be present in all you do. Savor each moment of your life; observe the world, the people in it, and the beauty that surrounds and resides within you.

g. Never Discount the Potential of Others.

A young female student of mine struggled in her academic pursuits. She often finished in the lower third of her class. As a result, she barely qualified for graduation. I hadn't seen her for years, until one day, while walking downtown, we met each other. I was surprised to learn that she was the Managing Director of one of the country's largest, most well-known off-shore financial institutions. Life is the cradle of hope and potential. Anyone, at any given moment, can transform their lives and reach their full potential. Stories of dramatic, seemingly overnight transformations abound, often spurred by significant, life-altering events. Therefore, never write people off, no matter how grim their current reality may appear.

h. Initiate Change Within Yourself.

People often lament the state of the world and yearn for change. However, when asked to be the pioneers of that change, they react with incredulity. The world outside is a reflection of our inner selves, and the chaos we observe is a manifestation of our collective consciousness. If we seek change, we must start by looking within. There are aspects within each of us – you, me, everyone – that warrant change.

i. Gratitude Paves the Way For More Blessings.

The law of attraction applies equally to both positive and negative aspects of our lives. It is up to us whether we focus on the adversities or the blessings. We could live as victims of our past or masters of our destiny. By expressing gratitude for what we have, we create a positive focus, inviting the universe to give us more reasons to be grateful.

Parting Thoughts

As I write the concluding words of this book, I reflect on a life filled with exploration, transformation, and resilience. A journey that was often challenging, but always worthwhile. Today, I find myself in a tranquil harbor, a testament to life's boundless possibilities, appreciating the calm after the storm.

I reflect on the milestones and individuals who have been integral to shaping my journey. I remember the strength found within, the lessons learned, and the faith that was my guiding light. Yet, this final chapter isn't about the turbulent past; but, rather, about the peaceful, auspicious present, and the promising horizons of the future.

At this juncture, it's impossible to overlook the significant role my life's directing principles and habits have played. While hope was the compass steering the journey, it also was the habits I developed and nurtured that gave me the ability to navigate the tumultuous seas of life. Habits like daily exercise, a disciplined spiritual practice, a commitment to clean and healthy eating – I haven't consumed meat for nearly forty years – and an enduring practice of forgiveness.

However, plumbing the depths of these vagaries has shown me that facing setbacks and continuing my journey is another story for another day. One focusing more on *practical* application. But for now, let's return to the serenity of my current shores.

In this stage of tranquility and contentment, one person shines brightly, my beloved wife, Michelle. The old saying, "The best is yet to come," has never resonated more deeply than when I think of the joy and serenity she has brought into my life.

Our love journey began earnestly in the fall of 2009, culminating in the exchange of solemn wedding vows on October 26, 2013 – and what a blessed, invigorating, growth-infused adventure it has been. As one elderly female member of my faith community once told me following Mass one Sunday morning as I sat in reverent silence before the Blessed Sacrament, "Son, you can go far in life, but you can go much further with a supportive wife." Her words, in the person of Michelle, are as true as she purposed.

Naturally, having endured two marriages, by 2007, I had entertained no thought of a third long-term relationship. My exclusive focus was the raising of my children, three of whom were in school at various levels.

But in the depths of my being, I also had to be honest with ME. While initially there was no interest in scouring the landscape of potential possibilities for a life-mate, I also knew that solitary life, devoid of a female partner, was not for me. Further, I also realized that, given the riveting focus on my parental responsibilities, and my unshakable determination to spiritual advancement, a suitably qualified partner had to be somebody who offered no impediments to either. Happily, God knew precisely who I needed, and in the person of my soul mate, I found her, Michelle.

This memoir tells the story of lessons hard-earned, and wisdom collected, set against the vibrant backdrop of the culture, politics, and personal experiences that shaped me. I've maneuvered through life understanding the importance of actions over mere words, the empowering act of teaching others how to treat me, the invaluable lessons in every mistake, and the liberation found in forgiveness. These pages encapsulate my life's journey, offering nuggets of wisdom along the way.

I invite you to understand that life isn't about resisting change, people, or circumstances, but rather, about appreciating the journey rather than fixating on the destination. It's not about writing people off, but recognizing that potential and hope thrive wherever life exists. It's about understanding that if we wish for the world to change, that change must begin first with us. Finally, it's about understanding the unequaled power of gratitude, and acknowledging that the more we express it, the more reasons the Universe gives us to be grateful.

In closing, the hope is that my story encourages you, illuminates your path, and perhaps even provides a compass as you steer your own unique pathway.

Remember, we each write our story.

This has been mine.

About the Author

Jeffrey Lloyd, hailing from New Providence, The Bahamas, stands out as a multifaceted leader with a diverse educational background from Nassau, the UK, the United States, and the Caribbean.

Throughout his journey, he has ventured into the realms of journalism, education, and law.

In May 2017, following a distinguished career spanning various domains, Jeffrey was elected as a Member of Parliament. Shortly after, on May 15, 2017, he was appointed Minister of Education in the Cabinet of the Bahamas.

Jeffrey is happily married to Michelle Donna Marie (nee Mitchell) and proudly holds the roles of both father and grandfather.

To learn more about Jeffrey and his endeavors, connect with him at his website: www.JeffreyLLloyd.com.

Acknowledgements

This seminal work is a labour of love that has spanned a decade. During that time, there were many who, having observed my life from a distance, encouraged me to not leave Earth before my life's story was documented somewhere. This is, in part, the fruit of that invitation.

I honour, firstly, the transcendent insights and impulse granted me through the Holy Spirit to vision and undertake this work. God be praised.

I have been additionally blessed with a supportive wife, Michelle; Daughters – Shiva, Aisha, Kendra, Sanjay, Shakti; Son, Alley, and a host of relatives and friends whose enabling support gave me the space to complete this undertaking. I am most especially indebted to a dear friend whose constant inspiration and motivation to get on with writing my book, Julie Hoyle, rung constantly in my ears. To her, I am grateful beyond words. When I didn't have the confidence to initiate this effort, she has been unwavering as a trusted guide, offering sage advice throughout my spiritual odyssey.

I am especially grateful to my publisher, Aisha, my eldest daughter, who's fast emerging as a genius in the publishing and literary disciplines. Her remarkably intuitive perceptions have been, indeed, stunning. The final stages and eventual publication of this book would not have been possible without her expert facility, patience, and wisdom.

May the words of these pages inflame passions within you to share your story with others.

UNIVERSAL IMPACT PRESS

Made in United States
Orlando, FL
07 February 2024